W9-DGK-232

ENDORSEMENTS

"I wish I had known these lessons from *Every Man a Warrior* in the early years of my marriage. It would have equipped me to do so much better as a husband and father. This study is a must for every man at any age. The material is tried and tested. It works! It is never too late to start building a better family!" *–Jerry E. White, Ph.D. and Chairman, U.S. Board of Directors, The Navigators*

"Men deal with issues every day that test their core values, integrity, and spiritual manhood. Issues like financial management, suffering, sex, moral purity, work, and making one's life count is the stuff that shapes a man's character. *Every Man a Warrior* hits these gut issues head on with no sugar coating." *–Lauren Libby, President and CEO of Trans World Radio International*

"In my 20-plus years of mentoring I've never seen one set of materials build men as effectively as *Every Man a Warrior.* I see this as a program I will do every year. It strengthens families and grows new leaders by building into the lives of the men in our church." *–Eric Matty, Associate Pastor, Real Life Church, St. Paul, MN*

"Lonnie, I took several hours tonight to read *Every Man a Warrior*. It is absolutely amazing and so full of practical wisdom. I praise God for the work he has done through you in the writing of this material. Now more than ever I hope thousands of men go through it. I know it will be transforming in their lives." *–Don Bartel, Navigator and U.S. Metro Ministry Leader.*

"In the past 15 years, I have worked with many different ministry materials designed to assist in discipling men. Some have been very good; however, all have been lacking a key step. None provided a well-designed method that would encourage and enable men to have a daily quiet time in God's Word.

That's the key in helping men's lives change. ***Every Man a Warrior*** has given me that missing step." *–John Degner, Metro Director, Christian Businessmen Connection (CBMC), Lincoln, NE*

"***Every Man a Warrior*** brings the disciple making process to where men live *'where the rubber meets the road.'* It teaches men how to apply biblical principals in managing money, marriage, and raising children. It helps them understand their wives, their woundedness, personal purity, integrity at work, and living for that which is eternal. ***Every Man a Warrior*** is a tool that gives men what they need to spiritually grow and become the husband, father, and man that God intended them to be." *–Jim Bender, Jim Bender Trucking Inc.*

Every Man a Warrior

HELPING MEN SUCCEED IN LIFE

Book 1

WALKING WITH GOD

BY LONNIE BERGER

NavPress
Discipleship Inside Out®

NavPress is the publishing ministry of The Navigators, an international Christian organization and leader in personal spiritual development. NavPress is committed to helping people grow spiritually and enjoy lives of meaning and hope through personal and group resources that are biblically rooted, culturally relevant, and highly practical.

For a free catalog go to www.NavPress.com
or call 1.800.366.7788 in the United States or 1.800.839.4769 in Canada.

EVERY MAN A WARRIOR is a ministry of The Navigators.

The Navigators are an interdenominational, nonprofit Christian organization, dedicated to discipling people **to know Christ and to make Him known.** *The Navigators have spiritually invested in people for over seventy-five years, coming alongside them one-on-one or in small groups to study the Bible, develop a deeper prayer life, and memorize the Scripture. Our ultimate goal is to equip men and women to fulfill the Great Commission of Matthew 28:19 to* **"Go and make disciples of all nations."** *Today, tens of thousands of people worldwide are coming to know and grow in Jesus Christ through the various ministries of The Navigators. Internationally, over 4,000 Navigator staff of 64 nationalities are serving in more than 100 countries.*

Learn more about The Navigators at www.navigators.org.

EVERY MAN A WARRIOR, BOOK 1: WALKING WITH GOD

© 2011 by The Navigators

All rights reserved. No part of this publication may be reproduced in any form without written permission from NavPress, P.O. Box 35001, Colorado Springs, CO 80935. www.navpress.com

NAVPRESS and the NAVPRESS logo are registered trademarks of NavPress. Absence of ® in connection with marks of NavPress or other parties does not indicate an absence of registration of those marks.

ISBN: 978-1-935-65122-2

Some of the anecdotal illustrations in this book are true to life and are included with permission of the persons involved. All other illustrations are composites of real situations, and any resemblance to people living or dead is coincidental.

Unless otherwise identified, all Scripture quotations in this publication are taken from the Holy Bible, New International Version® (NIV®). Copyright © 1973, 1978, 1984 Biblica. Used by permission of Zondervan. All rights reserved. Other versions used include: Revised Standard Version of the Bible (RSV), copyright 1946, 1952, 1971, by the Division of Christian Education of the National Council of the Churches of Christ in the USA, used by permission, all rights reserved; the New American Standard Bible® (NASB), Copyright © 1960, 1962, 1963, 1968, 1971, 1972, 1973, 1975, 1977, 1995 by The Lockman Foundation. Used by permission.

Printed in the United States of America.

2 3 4 5 6 7 8 9 10 / 17 16 15 14 13 12

You may download and reproduce any of the resources from the website EveryManAWarrior.com. These have been provided by the author for your benefit.

EVERY MAN A WARRIOR
Helping Men Succeed in Life

EVERY MAN A WARRIOR is a discipleship course designed to help men succeed in life. It is for men who want to become the warriors God intends—not living lives of mediocrity, but maturing and becoming equipped in the areas where men fight and need to win.

These areas include:
- Walking with God
- Marriage
- Raising Children
- Managing Money
- Going Through Hard Times
- Work
- Sex and Moral Purity
- Making Your Life Count

Overview of the *Every Man a Warrior* Series

EVERY MAN A WARRIOR is a discipleship Bible Study series for men comprised of three books. Here is how the course is put together:

Book 1 Walking with God

The first nine lessons of EVERY MAN A WARRIOR develop the essential skills of discipleship. These skills are: Having a Quiet Time, Meditating on Scripture, Prayer, and Application of the Word. These skills are then applied to the topics in the next two books. It is important that all men go through Book 1 before starting Books 2 and 3. Book 1 includes the EVERY MAN A WARRIOR verse pack and all course verses.

Book 2 Marriage and Raising Children

These eight lessons give practical help and a biblical outlook on both Marriage and Raising Children. It comes with a special emphasis on raising teenagers. These lessons have profoundly impacted the lives of men wanting to become better husbands and fathers.

Book 3 Money, Sex, Work, Hard Times, Making Your Life Count

Book 3 has ten lessons that bring scriptural application to the issues of Money, Work, Sex and Moral Purity, Going Through Hard Times, and How to Make Your Life Count. After family, these are the issues that most consume a man's life and where he needs to succeed.

Single men may choose to use only Books 1 and 3.

How to Use This Study

EVERY MAN A WARRIOR is designed for both married and single men. Each man needs to start with *Book 1.* It focuses on the discipleship skills and the process necessary to walk with God for a lifetime.

Those skills will then be used to develop biblical convictions, practical wisdom, and understanding in the next two books. If you are in a group of married men you will follow the course design order. Groups of single men can skip *Book 2, Marriage and Raising Children,* going immediately to *Book 3, Money, Work, Sex and Moral Purity, Going Through Hard Times, and How to Make Your Life Count.* If you have a mixed group of married and single men, go through all three books. Many single men want to study these topics also.

It can also work well to have men of different ages in the same group. Sometimes men in their fifties can share life lessons with men in their thirties that are helpful. This is not essential. Men in the same age group tend to bond more quickly, identifying with challenges they each face.

In a Small Group

Using *EVERY MAN A WARRIOR* in a small group of four to six men is optimum. These groups normally meet in the evening. Some groups have met successfully early on Saturday mornings or during the week before work. A time slot of ninety minutes is needed for groups.

One-on-One

The study can also be used to disciple men one-on-one, such as over lunch, and can be accomplished in sixty minutes.

A Men's Sunday School Class

EVERY MAN A WARRIOR can be used in a Sunday school class. However, this setting has some challenges if the class is less than an hour and has more than six men. Groups that meet in a Sunday school class will need to pair off and share quiet times and review verses in groups of two in order to save time starting with lesson five. Then the whole group comes back together to read the stories and discuss the lesson. Some lessons may take two weeks to complete, depending on the time allotted for your class. If used during a Sunday school class, make sure you keep your standards high and fulfill your "My Commitment" pledge on page 22.

How Every Man a Warrior Came About

This study comes from more than thirty years of discipleship experience while on staff with The Navigators. Over these years Lonnie Berger has worked to disciple, mentor, counsel, or train hundreds of men. The stories used in *EVERY MAN A WARRIOR* are all true. The names and some of the details have been changed to protect confidentiality and privacy.

Note to Leaders

Be sure to read "The Leader's Guide" on page 15 before your first meeting.

The first page of each lesson is for you, the leader. It is important to follow the Leader's Guide even if you have led other Bible studies. It has come from two years of field testing and is designed to help your group succeed. For example, some men find the disciplines of Quiet Times and Scripture memory hard to do and want to skip those parts of the course. ***Following the Leader's Guide will insure that these items are not left out and makes the Leader's Guide the course disciplinarian, not you!*** Not all groups make it and it is normal to have some men drop from the course. Using the Leader's Guide gives you the greatest potential to have a successful group.

CONTENTS

BOOK 1

APPENDIX

FOREWORD

Dear Men,

Our morally corrupt world has a tremendous, growing need for men to learn to love God with all their hearts. EVERY MAN A WARRIOR calls on men to grow into a deep, loving relationship with their heavenly Father. The framework of this study provides an excellent pathway for all who are ready to intensify their walk with Jesus.

As my friend and co-laborer Lonnie Berger says in the first lesson, not all men are ready to step into this process. It takes a great deal of commitment. But for those who long for new skills to strengthen their life of discipleship, this series provides an excellent framework.

Dallas Willard, Christian philosopher, professor, and author, says the spiritual disciplines are a way to put ourselves in a place to be taught by God's grace. The apostle Paul made a similar point in Philippians 2:12-13: *"Continue to work out your salvation with fear and trembling, for it is God who works in you to will and to act according to his good purpose."* God will do His work—but we must participate! This book, if the steps are followed and our hearts are open, will create such a learning environment for men.

In my experience, men in almost every church long for spiritual growth, but in many cases, the context for that development is missing. What churches need is a pathway that will motivate men to follow God. I believe that Lonnie has developed a well-designed process—smartly paced with solid, practical content—to meet that need.

Lonnie approaches tough life issues squarely, but with grace and humility. I love the way he puts his stories together in practical and encouraging ways. Yet he doesn't beat around the bush! He calls us to a clear-cut life of discipleship.

I am confident that men who commit to work through *EVERY MAN A WARRIOR* will be profoundly changed. There is nothing as powerful as the light of God's Word being brought to bear on the life of a man—and few things as influential as a man following hard after God in his personal life, his marriage, and in his finances.

I am so grateful to have read the *EVERY MAN A WARRIOR* series. Encouraged and challenged to follow God anew, I pray that God will raise up a generation of men who are strengthened by His power and filled with the fullness of God (Ephesians 3:14-21).

Alan Andrews
Former U.S. Director, The Navigators

PROLOGUE

I will never forget the fear that gripped my heart when I heard these words, *"Fire, fire! Take only your passports!"*

My first assignment with The Navigators was in 1980 as an undercover missionary in Romania. Nicolai Ceausescu was the communist dictator who ruled the country with an iron fist. Later, he was shot by his countrymen in 1989. Romania was one of the worst countries for Christians and was used by the Russians as a testing ground on how to deal with them. If a technique crushed the Christians in Romania, it was exported to other Eastern European communist countries.

Romania was a poor country with less than 5 percent of the people owning cars. During the food crisis of the early 1980s, each person was allotted seven eggs, a kilo of flour, a kilo of meat, and two liters of cooking oil per month.

The Navigators had run a secret travel ministry out of Vienna, Austria, for five years before I arrived. Different teams of people traveled each month to one of six different countries behind the iron curtain. To avoid the suspicion of the secret police, they changed their passports regularly and usually were not in one country more than twice a year.

The strategy had worked. More than 200 Romanian Christians from six cities had gone through a two-year course in discipleship. They met in private homes, away from the eyes of the secret police. But few people were coming to Christ. It was hard for the Romanians to share Christ, something they had not seen modeled, and there was the added fear of being sent to prison if caught or even accused of sharing their faith.

When I arrived in Vienna, I was asked to live inside Romania to train believers in sharing the gospel. A Christian professor at Kansas State University wrote me a letter of intent, and I was accepted to study "Socialistic Agriculture" at Babas Bolia University in Cluj-Napoca. The Lord blessed and later we saw some forty people come to Christ.

I lived in a student dorm with twelve floors, no elevators, and no fire escapes. I was on the ninth floor. When the alarm of fire came from another student, I could tell from the fear in his voice that this was serious. I raced to the door and saw the thick smoke layer clinging to the hallway ceiling. It was January. I grabbed my heavy coat, passport, and the little Bible that I had smuggled in and ran to the stairs.

The stairwell was our only way down and the smoke's only way up. By the sixth floor it was pitch black and we gagged on the smoke. Windows were painted shut. Students used chairs to break the glass in order to breathe. Students from all twelve floors were fleeing into the small space. The stairwell became a mass of screaming men, shoving and fighting to get fresh air.

By the time I reached the fourth floor I thought I was going to die. I shot up a prayer and said, *"Lord, thank You that I had the privilege to know You and to give my life to helping these people come to Christ."* As more students piled into the stairwell, we were driven down the stairs. The fire was contained on the first floor but the heat and flames blocked our exit. We were cut off.

Like rats on a burning ship, we jumped from the second-story window.

The ragged edges of broken glass were like saw teeth on the window. Somehow by the grace of God, I had on my winter gloves. Crawling out the window, I hung by my hands from the sill and let myself fall. I was scared but unhurt. Other students were bleeding, some with broken bones. We watched for thirty minutes as the building burned, hoping everyone had gotten out.

Then a student, horror frozen on his face, stuck his head out of the shattered window of the eighth floor. He was trying to descend. We watched helplessly as he came down, floor by floor, sticking his head out each window gasping for air. At the fourth floor the heat and flames were too intense. He panicked, crawled out on the window sill, slipped—and fell to his death.

The memory of his body falling in free space—against the backdrop of the burning building—is still seared into my brain. I thought to myself, *That could have been me!*

Men, we are all going to die! I find that every man, Christian or not, deep down on the inside wonders, *When I die will I have accomplished anything? Will my life have made a difference?*

LESSON 1

WHY DISCIPLESHIP

NOTE TO LEADERS

You can download the Leader's Guide from the web page at *www.EveryManAWarrior.com* to make it easier to follow while leading the lesson.

The website has a pdf with some thoughts on how to effectively lead a group. It is titled, *How to Start and Lead a Group.* As the leader, read these pages before your first meeting.

WHY DISCIPLESHIP?

The focus of this first session is to get acquainted and for each man to commit himself to the objective: *"To become the man God wants him to be!"*

✓ Hand out the books and let the men examine them.

✓ If the men do not know each other, spend the first few minutes getting each other's names, where they work, and family information. Give each man two minutes to share.

✓ Page 12-13: Read the *Prologue* together. Go around the circle and have each man read a paragraph or two.

✓ Pages 16–24: Read *Why Discipleship?* Whenever there is a ✓ it means there is a question to discuss. Stop at each ✓ and ask the questions.

✓ Page 24: Read *Points to Remember* and the *Assignment.*

✓ Go around the room and record each man's contact information in the *Contact Information* page at the back of the book.

✓ Choose a time and place to meet.

✓ The leader should end in prayer.

To Fight and End Well

Few Christian men end well. They start out with zeal for the things of God and then begin to coast. Finally, they compromise and many finish their lives with regret.

As Christian men we are constantly engaged in a war. Whether we realize it or not, our life is the battlefield and Satan our enemy.

As long as you are a non-Christian, the Enemy for the most part leaves you alone. He has already won. But when you accept and know Christ, the battle is on. Now you are a threat to Satan's kingdom and he begins to fight. The more you grow in Christ, the brighter your light pierces through Satan's veil of darkness. The Enemy is exposed; your joy is attractive to others. The Devil must work to discredit you.

So why is it that so many Christian men end poorly? *I believe that most men have never been trained and equipped with the necessary skills to fight and end well.* If no soldier ever went through boot camp, what percentage do you think would make it through a battle?

This course is designed to equip men with these essential skills. If you are a man, either now or somewhere in the future you will struggle with the following challenges: *walking consistently with God, managing your money wisely, marriage, raising your children, facing hard times, your work and career, staying morally pure, and making your life count!*

Most men have never been trained and equipped with the skills necessary to fight and end well.

These are the battlefields where men spend the majority of their lives. It's also where the Enemy attacks. Unfortunately, many of us lack good role models or practical teaching in these subjects. If we are not skilled to fight, most of us will lose. This course is designed to give you those indispensable skills to fight, win, and end your life well!

✓ What do you think of the statement that, "most men have never been equipped with the skills necessary to fight and win" in the areas mentioned above?

✓ In which of the following areas do you look forward to being better trained: Walking consistently with God, managing your money wisely, marriage, raising your children, facing hard times, your work and career, staying morally pure, and making your life count? List them.

WHY DISCIPLESHIP?

Jesus was a builder of men—men of great courage. Eleven of the twelve apostles died as martyrs. James was the first to be killed; Peter was crucified upside down on a cross. Paul was imprisoned, beaten, shipwrecked, stoned, whipped, and eventually beheaded.

These followers of Christ were real men. They were men with backbone and strength of character, willing to die for something they believed in. There was nothing wimpy about these guys. *How do you build men like that today?*

When my father-in-law was dying of cancer, he asked me to stay a few minutes alone by his side. In our conversation, he said things I will never forget. It was our last time to talk, and his words had a profound impact on my life.

Last words are like that. Jesus' last words also have extraordinary implications. His specific command was meant to give his followers a strategy. *"Go and make disciples!"*

> **"All authority in heaven and on earth has been given to me. Therefore go and make disciples of all nations, . . . teaching them to obey everything I have commanded you."**
>
> — *Matthew 28:18-20*

The word *"make"* implies building something. It means to construct, to fabricate, to produce, or bring about. It presupposes that there are *specific ingredients* and a *well-defined process*.

When my daughters were beginning to cook, they liked to make cakes. It was a learning process. Put in the wrong ingredients and you get something inedible. Not a cake! Forget the process; leave your cake in the oven for five hours at 400 degrees and you get a brick. *Also not a cake!*

It's exactly the same with discipleship. Discipleship requires that exact essential elements be used or we are not making biblical disciples. Use the wrong elements or an ineffective process and the transforming power of discipleship is sabotaged.

But Jesus did not set us up for failure. No, he gave a clear description of what "making disciples" means! His definition was and still is "teaching them to obey everything" Jesus had taught them.

What Jesus focused on during his three years with the twelve disciples is not that difficult to discover. In lessons 1 through 9 we will uncover the essential elements of discipleship that Jesus gave and the skills that go with them. I call them "The Building Blocks of Discipleship."

Watering down the standards of discipleship hurts the building of men!

THE ROLE OF STANDARDS IN THE DISCIPLESHIP PROCESS

Now let's talk a little about the discipleship process. For five years with The Navigators, I did church consulting. Churches paid me to help them develop their adult discipleship programs.

In 90 percent of the cases when the people did the work outlined in the program we developed, their lives began to change. The time they spent with Jesus began to give them a sense of joy and purpose they had never experienced. In one church we started with men only. After a few months a wife or two approached me and said, "I don't know what you are doing with my husband, but he's changed. Keep it up!"

In each of the churches I discovered an interesting stumbling block. Three to four weeks into the process, someone would approach me confidentially and say, "You know, we don't want to make the requirements too high for this group. Someone may not be able to do the work. We certainly don't want to exclude or offend anyone. Do we?"

Many times I saw this attitude saturating all their church programs. The inclination was to set the bar low so that no one was excluded or felt left out. In some church activities this is exactly the way it should be. Sunday school classes or small groups that are safe, compassionate, and minister to those hurting and struggling among us are good examples of when inclusiveness is needed.

But that mentality kills the building of men, and it destroys the discipleship process. If you are going to bring men to maturity, they have to be challenged. You don't build character and leadership skills by watering down the requirements. You don't send men into war without rigorous training and specific skills and expect them to win.

✓ Why do you think watering down the standards of discipleship hurts the building of men?

BUILDING BLOCKS OF DISCIPLESHIP

Many other building blocks could be listed in the following illustration. God's specific calling on your life will determine what they are. But if a man is to be a disciple, walk with God for a lifetime, and fulfill his calling, then the Building Blocks of Discipleship must be firmly in place.

By the grace God has given me, I laid a foundation as an expert builder.
—1 Corinthians 3:10

Some churches have focused so much on including everyone in every church event that the spiritual maturity of the church is anemic. But healthy churches, while ministering to the hurt and struggling, also have an intentional focus on discipling some men for future leadership. This group is not open to everyone. It has standards that guarantee growth.

Disciple just 10 percent of the men in your church, challenge them to walk with God, and it will have a ripple effect. It will raise the spiritual

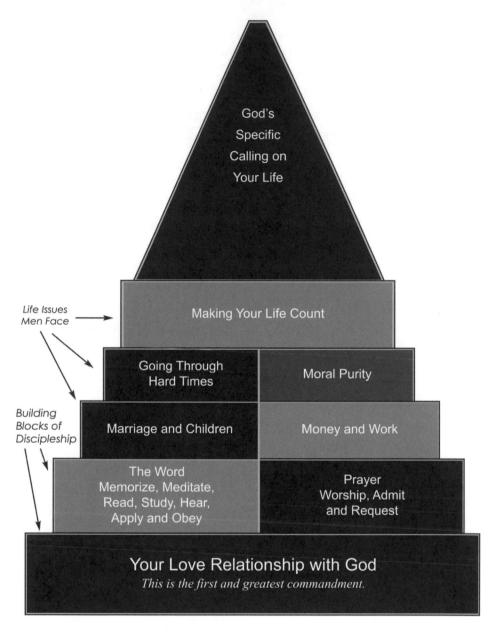

God's
Specific
Calling on
Your Life

*Life Issues
Men Face* →

Making Your Life Count

Going Through
Hard Times

Moral Purity

*Building
Blocks of
Discipleship*

Marriage and Children

Money and Work

The Word
Memorize, Meditate,
Read, Study, Hear,
Apply and Obey

Prayer
Worship, Admit
and Request

Your Love Relationship with God
This is the first and greatest commandment.

THE BUILDING BLOCKS OF DISCIPLESHIP

watermark of the whole church. And in a few years it means the church has more available workers to carry the load.

It is important to note that Jesus ministered to the masses. In fact He responded to their hurts, sorrows, and brokenness with compassion. But He also focused on building twelve men to be leaders who could someday be workers, ministering to the masses. With His disciples He didn't water down the standards. No, He challenged them regularly to see if they were up to the task.

In John 6:66-68, after Jesus had taught on a hard issue—living for the eternal rather than the temporal—some of His disciples grumbled. Jesus didn't seem to be upset. He knew that if these men were to be the future leaders of a movement that would transform the world, they had to make a choice. Would they live for what was eternal, or did they want to live for things that would someday mean nothing at all? In fact, Jesus still gives us that same choice today!

> *From this time many of his disciples turned back and no longer followed him. "You do not want to leave too, do you?" Jesus asked the Twelve. Simon Peter answered him, "Lord, to whom shall we go? You have the words of eternal life."*
>
> —*John 6:66-68*

This course does have requirements. At the peak of expectations, it requires that you spend twenty to thirty minutes five days a week in the Scriptures or preparing for the lesson. It also asks that you meet once a week with your group. Hopefully you can make this the highest priority for your Christian activities. You may need to pull back from some other responsibilities. This will allow you to grow in your spiritual maturity now so that you can bear more fruit later.

For many men who have gone through the discipleship process, it becomes the most meaningful and fruitful time ever in their Christian lives. I remember the head elder at one church who beamed with excitement when he said, "Lonnie, because of the discipleship training, I've grown more in the last six months than in the previous six years!"

THE ROLE OF ACCOUNTABILITY IN THE DISCIPLESHIP PROCESS

In our society the predominant philosophy of "personal autonomy" is epidemic. The attitude that no one has the right to tell me what to do, or hold me to any standard other than what I choose, is rampant. Unfortunately, in our society of "no moral absolutes," personal autonomy also means anarchy and lawlessness.

Accountability is a good thing, and few men walk with God for a lifetime without it.

But the Scripture says that the right kind of accountability is not a bad thing. It's a good thing, meant to help us achieve our goals. In discipleship, accountability is intended to help you be a better man. It is designed for the context of a safe environment where men determine to help each other become what God wants them to be. Accountability is a good thing, and few men walk with God for a lifetime without it.

In war the objective is to stay alive—to kill the enemy before he kills you. So soldiers go through extensive training. They are stripped of their personal autonomy in order to learn to fight together as a team, but with each man carrying his own weight.

The Christian life is similar. It is definitely a war. Our enemy the Devil has one objective, to "steal and kill and destroy" (John 10:10). In 1 Peter 5:8 he says, "Your enemy the devil prowls around like a roaring lion looking for someone to devour." This sounds like war to me.

My Commitment

In order to become more the man that God wants me to be, I commit myself to the following:

1. I will make weekly attendance at the meeting a priority.
2. I will complete the assignment for the week and be willing to share my thoughts with the group.
3. I will hold in confidence any personal matter shared in the group.
4. I will encourage my brothers to be courageous, do the work, and become the men that God wants them to be.
5. I will not be defensive if my brothers challenge me if I do not fulfill my commitment. I will welcome their challenge and seek greater faithfulness.

Signed _____

Date _____

✓ How do you feel about the role of keeping high standards in the discipleship training process?

✓ Discuss as a group what it means to sign the commitment on page 22.

✓ Discuss the verse below, Ecclesiastes 4:9-10. How important is accountability in accomplishing goals in life? How important is accountability in starting new spiritual habits?

✓ What has been your track record on keeping personal commitments when you did not have accountability?

Two are better than one, because they have a good return for their work: If one falls down his friend can help him up. But pity the man who falls and has no one to help him up!

—Ecclesiastes 4:9-10

Points to Remember

1. Jesus gave us HIS definition of discipleship. We need to teach what HE taught.

2. You cannot disciple men and prepare them for leadership by lowering the standards. Keeping the standards high and doing the work ensures that men will grow.

3. Accountability is important for men to grow spiritually, and few men walk with God for a lifetime without it.

Before Leaving the Meeting

✓ Choose a place and time to meet.

✓ Exchange phone numbers and e-mail addresses in order to be able to contact each other. Use the *Contact Information* page at the back of the book.

ASSIGNMENT FOR NEXT WEEK

1. Complete lesson 2 and be ready to discuss your thoughts at the next meeting.

2. Since we only remember 10 percent of what we read, keep a pen in hand to underline, jot notes, or ask questions when reading the lesson.

3. Sign and date *My Commitment* on page 22.

Leader's Guide to

LESSON 2
FINDING THE "ONE THING"

NOTE TO LEADERS

You can download the Leader's Guide from the website *www.EveryManAWarrior.com* to make it easier to follow while leading the lesson.

FINDING THE "ONE THING"

✓ Open the session with prayer. We will start praying as a group in lesson 7.

✓ Ask if everybody completed the lesson.

✓ Ask if everyone signed the *My Commitment* pledge on page 22. If not, ask them to do so now.

✓ Ask someone to start reading the lesson, and go around the circle, each man reading a paragraph or two. *Whenever there is a ✓ it means there is a question to discuss.* Stop at each ✓ and ask the questions.

✓ Pages 26-35: Ask each of the questions on these pages. Depending on time, have two to four people give their answer. Try to include everyone.

✓ Page 34: Have each person share what he wrote for his Quiet Time on Colossians 3. Make sure they follow the guidelines from *How to Share Your Quiet Time with the Group.*

✓ Page 35-36: Read the *Points to Remember* and the *Assignment*.

✓ Remind them that next week they will share from their Quiet Times.

✓ End in prayer, asking the Lord to help these men develop their skill in having Quiet Times.

FINDING THE "ONE THING"

In the 1991 hit comedy *City Slickers*, Mitch and his two best friends are each confronted with a midlife crisis. Mitch, played by Billy Crystal, hates his dead-end job. His friends Phil and Ed, played by Daniel Stern and Bruno Kirby, have their own dilemmas. Phil is trapped in a sexless marriage to an overbearing wife. Ed, a playboy and businessman, is wondering if he will ever have a meaningful permanent relationship with a wife and children.

At Mitch's thirty-ninth birthday party, Phil and Ed present their gift: a two-week cattle drive in the Southwest. The cattle drive is presented as a solution to the question that is overwhelming each man: *What really is the meaning and purpose of life?*

Into this journey rides Jack Palance as Curly. This self-reliant, tough-as-nails trail boss chastises the three city slickers for wasting their lives because they have not yet discovered the *"One Thing!"*

Mitch is terrified of Curly—yet drawn to his confidence and focused life. In a hilarious experience, Mitch and Curly battle together to deliver a newborn calf. This rare bonding experience creates a confiding moment between the two men when Curly begins to share the source of his self-confidence. *"You've got to discover the 'One Thing,'"* Curly explained. *"Without it your life is always messed up."*

Mitch rushes back to his companions. With excitement, he tells his friends how Curly knows the "One Thing." Mitch assures them that Curly will definitely share the secret of life's purpose. Their lives will no longer be meaningless! They are at the end of their quest! Tomorrow they will solve the puzzle of life, the "One Thing."

But that night Curly dies. The secret to life's purpose is lost again!

Do you know the *"One Thing"?* There is one thing in life that is above all others and gives purpose and meaning even when life is horrible, as it sometimes is. God designed you for this one purpose, and without it life is meaningless. The next few pages could radically change your life forever. *Read on with expectation!*

✓ How important is it to know that your life will count for something significant?

THE FIRST BUILDING BLOCK OF DISCIPLESHIP IS THE "ONE THING!"

Last week we described discipleship as having essential elements, or building blocks. Jesus was certainly a builder of men. *The first building block of discipleship is the "One Thing,"* and it's found in the story of Matthew 22:34-38.

Loving God is the foundational cornerstone of your whole Christian life.

✓ Read Matthew 22:34-38 below.

Jesus was getting all the press. The religious establishment was trying to undermine Him—and sent a lawyer to test Him. The lawyer may have been thinking about the Ten Commandments. Whatever commandment Jesus would choose, the lawyer could argue that one of the other nine was more important.

But Jesus exploded their paradigm. He did not talk about ten rules. He gave us a glimpse into the very heart of God by revealing *God's eternal purpose: a love relationship with each of us.*

God loves you, and His greatest desire is that you would know Him intimately. He wants you to know Him so well that you start to perceive His love and begin to love Him back.

All the religions of the world except Christianity are based on sets of rules. But Jesus and His Father want a relationship with you and me. This truth is indescribable, amazing, and awesome. It is the *"One Thing."*

Hearing that Jesus had silenced the Sadducees, the Pharisees got together. One of them, an expert in the law, tested him with this question: "Teacher, which is the greatest commandment in the Law?"
Jesus replied: "Love the Lord your God with all your heart and with all your soul and with all your mind. This is the first and greatest commandment."

Matthew 22:34-38

✓ Take a minute and read the Matthew 22 passage again.

To develop a love relationship with God, we must spend time with Him.

In verses 37 and 38 Jesus says that loving God is not only the greatest commandment but the first as well. It's the greatest—this suggests the most important, or that it has the biggest impact. It's the first—implying the highest priority, something we do before anything else. This passage describes "loving God" as the foundational cornerstone of your whole Christian life. In fact, if you and I get this right, everything else falls neatly into place and we build our lives on a foundation that will last for eternity.

If knowing and loving God with all our heart, soul, and mind is the most important thing we can do in life, *then how do we accomplish that?* It has to do with skills—and the lack of emphasis on building these skills into believers is one of the biggest blind spots of the church in America.

Let me illustrate the need for skills. I have two wonderful, beautiful daughters, now both grown. But just a few years ago they wanted to learn how to drive. The state of Nebraska required fifty hours of driving with an adult. First, we got the learner's permit and started driving in a big parking lot. Then we spent five hours over the next few days driving on some quiet neighborhood streets. We recorded every minute until each hour was completed. Eventually they graduated to busy streets and finally the interstate. Later I got a map of Omaha and said, "Take me to this address," and each learned how to navigate the city.

But why did I do it this way? Because developing a safe teenage driver is about *skills, skills, skills!* What would have happened if I had just lectured my daughters for fifty hours about driving a car? We could have read books, discussed the value of different auto makers, and talked until I was blue in the face about avoiding accidents. We all know what would have happened. They would have crashed during their first driving experience.

The Christian life is like that. It has to be experienced. In fact, to succeed, like driving, *you must give significant time and energy to develop your skills.*

✓ What do you think of Curly's statement? "You've got to discover the 'One Thing.' Without it your life is always messed up." Be prepared to share your thoughts.

✓ What are your thoughts about the need to develop skills in order to successfully live the Christian life?

In this lesson we discovered the *first and most important building block of discipleship: developing your love relationship with God.* Now, let's discover the skill needed to build this truth into your life.

To develop your love relationship with anyone, you must spend time with that person. The time has to be consistent and with a directed focus if the relationship is going to mature to a deeper level over time. *To develop a love relationship with God, we must spend time with Him.* It's called a *"Quiet Time,"* and there are skills that will determine its effectiveness.

✓ Do you believe the statement, "To develop a love relationship with God we must spend time with Him"? Why?

Now let's get started on your first skill with The ABCs of Quiet Time.

THE ABCS OF HAVING A QUIET TIME

A: Ask questions and record your thoughts and meditations.

Is there a commandment to obey?
Is there a promise to claim?
Is there a sin to avoid?
Is there an application to make?
Is there something new about God?

Each time you mark something in Scripture, ask yourself these questions to stimulate your thinking.

B: After meditating, choose a Best Verse and write it down. Record your Best Thoughts on this verse.

The "B" is the most crucial element in having an effective Quiet Time.

The "A" of Ask questions is like the many pellets of a shotgun shell. But the "B" of Best Verse and Best Thought is like a single rifle bullet that hits the bull's-eye of a target.

C: Communicate back to the Lord in prayer whatever you feel He is impressing on you. (We will examine prayer in depth in lessons 6 and 7.)

IMPORTANT QUIET TIME GUIDELINES

1. Choose a time and place to have a daily Quiet Time. Most men choose the morning. Depending on your schedule, you may find that before bed works best. Choose a place that will keep you free from interruption or distraction.

2. Use the Quiet Time Journal to record your thoughts. Writing down your thoughts forces you to think and helps the Scripture to take root more deeply in you. This process will transform your life. The Enemy really fights against this.

3. Start a new lifelong habit. Do not be discouraged if you find this hard. This will take time to establish and will challenge your priorities. But it is worth the cost. Someday you will look back and realize that your most cherished moments on earth were times spent with the Lord.

✓ Review the A and B definitions above. How are they different? Why is B the most crucial element of having an effective Quiet Time? What are your thoughts?

Having a daily Quiet Time is a skill. This skill will take time and effort, but it will determine your success or failure. Give it your best! Your Quiet Time will grow over time. Most men shoot for thirty minutes, but you can start with fifteen minutes:

* 5 minutes to read and underline
* 7 minutes to meditate and write in your Quiet Time Journal
* 3 minutes to pray
* The Bible is a library of sixty-six books. If you are new to Bible reading, start in the New Testament with one of the Gospels. Then read the book of Acts. After you have read four or five books in the New Testament, try the Old Testament books of Genesis, Proverbs, or the Psalms.

THE QUIET TIME

Attention: You must read the following instructions to complete the lesson.

1. Take a few minutes to read Colossians 3:1-17 on pages 32 and 33. With pen in hand, underline, circle, or highlight any part of the passage that seems especially important to you.

2. Jot down one or two major themes from Colossians 3:1-17 in the Quiet Time box (page 34).

3. Choose one verse from this passage that spoke to you. This is your "Best Verse" for the day.

4. Try to do the "A" part. Ask the questions listed on your Best Verse. What thoughts come to mind?

5. Try the "B" part of Quiet Time. Write out your "Best Verse" and your "Best Thought" in the place provided. Be prepared to share what you wrote with the group.

6. Circle any appropriate "Ask" questions that apply.

7. Use the Quiet Time sample provided from Matthew 22:34-40 as a guide (bottom, page 34).

8. We will share our Quiet Times with the group when we get to page 35 and read "How to Share your Quiet Time with the Group."

Colossians 3:1-17

[1]Since, then, you have been raised with Christ, set your hearts on things above, where Christ is seated at the right hand of God. [2]Set your minds on things above, not on earthly things. [3]For you died, and your life is now hidden with Christ in God. [4]When Christ, who is your life, appears, then you also will appear with him in glory.

[5]Put to death, therefore, whatever belongs to your earthly nature: sexual immorality, impurity, lust, evil desires and greed, which is idolatry. [6]Because of these, the wrath of God is coming.

[7]You used to walk in these ways, in the life you once lived. [8]But now you must rid yourselves of all such things as these: anger, rage, malice, slander, and filthy language from your lips. [9]Do not lie to each other, since you have taken off your old self with its practices [10]and have

EVERY MAN A WARRIOR

put on the new self, which is being renewed in knowledge in the image of its Creator. ¹¹Here there is no Greek or Jew, circumcised or uncircumcised, barbarian, Scythian, slave or free, but Christ is all, and is in all.

¹²Therefore, as God's chosen people, holy and dearly loved, clothe yourselves with compassion, kindness, humility, gentleness and patience. ¹³Bear with each other and forgive whatever grievances you may have against one another. Forgive as the Lord forgave you. ¹⁴And over all these virtues put on love, which binds them all together in perfect unity.

¹⁵Let the peace of Christ rule in your hearts, since as members of one body you were called to peace. And be thankful. ¹⁶Let the word of Christ dwell in you richly as you teach and admonish one another with all wisdom, and as you sing psalms, hymns and spiritual songs with gratitude in your hearts to God. ¹⁷And whatever you do, whether in word or deed, do it all in the name of the Lord Jesus, giving thanks to God the Father through him.

Date_____ Passage I Read Today_____

Major themes from all I read.

_____

_____

Best verse and thought for the day. (Write the verse & your thoughts.)

_____

_____

_____

_____

Ask Questions

Is there:

A command to obey

A promise to claim

A sin to avoid

An application to make

Something new about God

Ask: Who, What, When, Where, Why

Emphasize: Different words

Rewrite: In your own words

Communicate *With God*

W *- Worship Him*

A *- Admit Sin*

R *- My Requests*

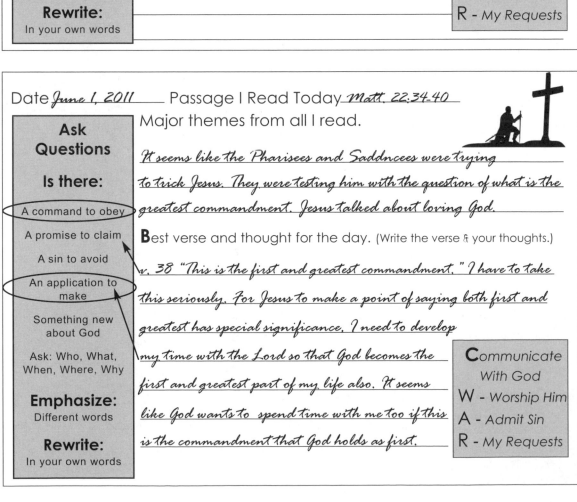

Date *June 1, 2011* ___ Passage I Read Today *Matt. 22:34-40*

Major themes from all I read.

It seems like the Pharisees and Sadducees were trying to trick Jesus. They were testing him with the question of what is the greatest commandment. Jesus talked about loving God.

Best verse and thought for the day. (Write the verse & your thoughts.)

v. 38 "This is the first and greatest commandment." I have to take this seriously. For Jesus to make a point of saying both first and greatest has special significance. I need to develop my time with the Lord so that God becomes the first and greatest part of my life also. It seems like God wants to spend time with me too if this is the commandment that God holds as first.

Ask Questions

Is there:

A command to obey

A promise to claim

A sin to avoid

An application to make

Something new about God

Ask: Who, What, When, Where, Why

Emphasize: Different words

Rewrite: In your own words

Communicate *With God*

W *- Worship Him*

A *- Admit Sin*

R *- My Requests*

HOW TO SHARE YOUR QUIET TIME WITH THE GROUP

Sometimes when Christians share their thoughts from the Bible with each other, they are tempted to preach or explain great spiritual mysteries. However, to save time we will share our Quiet Times each week in this way:

1. Cite the passage you read so that people can turn to it and follow along.

2. Share your major themes from the passage.

3. Read the Best Verse and your Best Thoughts from your Quiet Time.

4. Share any "Ask Questions" that you circled.

5. Follow the example at the bottom of page 34.

✓ Now have each person in the group share his Quiet Time from Colossians 3.

Points to Remember

1. Developing your love relationship with the Lord is the most important, significant, essential objective you can have in life. It is the *"One Thing."* It is the first and most foundational building block of every aspect of your Christian life. (See page 20.)

2. Having a daily Quiet Time is a skill that needs to be developed. This skill will take time and effort, but it will determine your success or failure.

3. The *ABCs of Quiet Time* will help you not just do a spiritual activity, but also develop a meaningful time of fellowship with the God of the universe. *"I want to spend enough time with Jesus every day that my heart gets glad."*—Martin Luther

EVERY MAN A WARRIOR

ASSIGNMENT FOR NEXT WEEK

1. Choose a time and place for you to have a daily Quiet Time. If you are new to Bible reading, start in the New Testament with one of the Gospels. Then read the book of Acts. After you have read four or five books in the New Testament, try the Old Testament books of Genesis, Proverbs, or the Psalms.

2. Have three Quiet Times using the ABCs and record them in your Quiet Time Journal in the back of the book. Be prepared to share one Quiet Time with the rest of the group. Use 1 or 2 additional Quiet Times to do your lesson.

3. You will need to have three written Quiet Times each week to complete the course requirements.

4. Come prepared having finished lesson 3. Read the lesson with a pen in hand to mark passages and jot down your thoughts.

Leader's Guide to

LESSON 3
WHY
MEN FAIL

NOTE TO LEADERS

It is important to follow the Leader's Guide while leading the lesson. While some items are the same each week, others are specific, one-time instructions that will negatively impact the study if missed. These items are marked with a star. ★

WHY MEN FAIL

✓ Open the session with prayer.

✓ Ask the group participants how they got along in their Quiet Times.

★✓ Go back and reread *How to Share Your Quiet Time with the Group* (page 35). We will share Quiet Times each week so it is important to get the skill right.

✓ Ask them to turn to their Quiet Time Journal and choose one Quiet Time they would like to share from this week.

★✓ After sharing Quiet Times, go back and reread the *ABCs of having a Quiet Time* and *Important Quiet Time Guidelines*, pages 29-31. This is a new lifelong habit, so let's review.

✓ Ask someone to start reading the lesson. Go around the circle, with each man reading a paragraph or two. *Whenever there is a ✓ it means there is a question to discuss.* Stop at each ✓ and ask the questions.

✓ Pages 40-43: Ask each of the questions on these pages. Depending on time, have two to four people give their answer. Try to include everyone.

✓ Page 43: Read John 15:4-8 as a group, then discuss each of the questions. Try to involve each man in sharing.

✓ Page 44: Read the *Points to Remember* and the *Assignment.*

✓ Pull out your *EMAW Verse Pack* and place Matthew 22:36-38 in the front window.

✓ End the time in prayer asking God to help each of the men in their Quiet Times.

LEADER'S GUIDE

WHY MEN FAIL

It was January, 1980, when I stepped off the train into the frigid air of Vienna, Austria. I was filled with anticipation—the beginning of my first missionary assignment. It took a few days to get settled, and then I began preparation for my first trip into Romania.

Jimmy Carter was president and had made a connection between human rights and Favored Nations Status with communist countries in Eastern Europe. If word got out that Christians were being persecuted, it could derail a country's status as a Favored Nation and affect their ability to get dollars or badly needed technology from the West. Only a few of our missionaries traveling as tourists had been detained, strip-searched, or barred at the border. But we knew there was always a risk.

One group of American pastors brought some U.S. lawyers to Romania. After preaching in a few churches, the pastors with their lawyers made complaints about the treatment of Christians. In the middle of the night they were hauled from their beds by the secret police, slapped around, and promptly put on an airplane back to America. We wanted to operate differently. We bought Romanian clothes and kept our mouths shut to avoid being noticed.

A year earlier, our first U.S. Navigator staff member had obtained a visa to study in Romania. John was an art major, twenty-seven years old, with a gift for languages. His visa permitted him to live in the country and study beautiful religious paintings in Greek Orthodox churches. With his access to cathedrals, it was natural for him to meet with me covertly in one of the most significant tourist attractions of the country—an unused 200-year-old Greek Orthodox cathedral.

During my first trip, John and I traveled the country, meeting with our Christian contacts in six cities. We were training the city leaders in discipleship, and they were secretly leading some 200 Romanian Christians to study the Bible, have Quiet Times, and memorize the Word.

Except for being with the believers, it was a sobering trip. We saw men and women weeping on the street because of food shortages. We observed firsthand the hopelessness of the communist system. In January, the cities of Romania seemed gray, drab, and cold.

The Christian men living in a communist country faced amazing challenges. It was against the law for Romanians to meet with foreigners, study the Bible together, or share their faith. They risked being sent to prison every time we met. One man had his house constantly watched by the secret police; others had their phones tapped. Still, they were willing to take the risk and were eager to meet with us. They developed a system of code words to communicate when it was safe to meet in their homes.

When we met in a believer's home they always wanted to serve us a meal. They divided the meat so that we got the largest portions. Sometimes they spent their whole month's ration of meat, about two pounds per person, on us. These believers were the most amazing example of love and self-sacrifice I had ever seen.

What's hard to absorb is that Christian men in America do not face extraordinary pressures, yet they have affairs, abandon their families, use pornography, or generally do nothing for God. According to George Barna, a leading U.S. researcher, Christian men in America get divorced just as often as men with no church background. His studies also show that 50% of men who call themselves Christians regularly use pornography. *Why do so many American Christian men fail?*

In 2009 at a men's conference in Omaha, Nebraska, conference speaker Steve Farrar shared this shocking research. He had interviewed more than 200 pastors who had fallen into disgrace by having affairs with women in their church. In doing the analysis, he discovered three deadly mistakes that virtually every man had made. They each admitted that in the twelve months before the affair started:

1. They had stopped having their Quiet Times.
2. They had stopped being accountable to other men for their Quiet Time.
3. They had counseled women behind closed doors.

A man's Quiet Time is perhaps the best barometer of the condition of his walk with God. When he is regular and consistent in feeding his soul and communing with God, his spiritual life is full of vitality. He's also protected. But when his time alone with God stops, he becomes spiritually anemic, vulnerable, and an easy target for the Enemy.

There is a relationship between a man's Quiet Time and his ability to handle stress, face a crisis, or do what's right when relationship challenges surface.

✓ Why do you think Christian men in America struggle in the Christian life? List at least two ideas.

There are many reasons a man does not have a consistent Quiet Time. But after thirty years of discipling, I have concluded there are three key reasons that impact the process of discipleship. They are applicable to Quiet Time, evangelism, discipleship, prayer, Scripture memory, fruitfulness, and many other aspects of the Christian life. We will first apply these reasons to our Quiet Time. If these issues are not effectively addressed in the *discipleship process,* the program will most likely fail.

THREE REASONS MEN FAIL IN THEIR QUIET TIME

Reason 1: No one ever taught them how to have a Quiet Time. It is a skill that needs to be taught, developed, and maintained.

In Lesson 2 we learned the ABCs of Quiet Time and practiced writing down our thoughts. Later we will learn about the art of meditation, asking questions, and translating verses into your own words. *Each method is a skill. The sharper your skills, the more effective your Quiet Time will become.*

If the ax is dull and its edge unsharpened, more strength is needed but skill will bring success.

—*Ecclesiastes 10:10 (emphasis added)*

Reason 2: Satan does not want you to have a successful Quiet Time.

Too many Christian men are ignorant of the daily war they are in. They get bushwhacked by the Enemy. Men know they need to develop disciplines to grow closer to God. They want to have a regular Quiet Time.

But it is hard to develop new habits and it doesn't happen.

I've heard this statement a hundred times: *"When I'm having my Quiet Time, it seems like all hell breaks loose in our house. The kids start crying, the phone rings, or my mind is flooded with details about things I need to do at the office."* Satan always tries to destroy your love relationship with the Lord. This is why a well-thought-out place and time for your Quiet Time is so important.

But I am afraid that just as Eve was deceived by the serpent's cunning, your minds may somehow be led astray from your sincere and pure devotion to Christ.

—2 Corinthians 11:3

Reason 3: Men have no one to hold them accountable in their Quiet Times.

Since we are at war, and the key to winning in the Christian life is the development of our time alone with God, accountability is absolutely essential. Many groups have no accountability standards. Some do not even ask that you do the lesson beforehand. If we are going to start a new lifelong habit that the Enemy is committed to defeat, we must have brothers who hold us accountable and gently pick us up when we fall.

Two are better than one, because they have a good return for their work: If one falls down, his friend can help him up. But pity the man who falls and has no one to help him up!

—Ecclesiastes 4:9-10

✓ Review the *Three Reasons Men Fail,* pages 40-41 and answer the following questions from the verses on these pages.

✓ *Reason 1:* Do you think that Quiet Time is a skill? Why?

✓ What principle is taught in Ecclesiastes 10:10?

✓ *Reason 2:* What are ways that the Enemy tries to defeat us?

✓ According to 2 Corinthians 11:3, from what does the Devil try to lead us astray? How does this connect with the first building block of discipleship?

✓ *Reason 3:* According to Ecclesiastes 4:9-10, why is accountability important in starting a new skill?

✓ If your walk with Christ begins to decline, do you want a brother to help you back up? What happens when a man stumbles spiritually and has no one to pick him up?

✓ What do you think of the statement: *"There is a relationship between a man's Quiet Time and his ability to handle stress, face a crisis, or do what's right when relationship challenges surface."* Record your thoughts. Be prepared to share with the group.

Take some time to do the ABCs of Quiet Time on the following passage. Review pages 29-30 if needed. Then answer the questions and be ready to discuss. Your version may use the word remain in the place of *abide.* Abide means "to *dwell or live in."* It can also mean *"to hold fast to."*

> *Abide in me, and I in you. As the branch cannot bear fruit by itself, unless it abides in the vine, neither can you, unless you abide in me. I am the vine, you are the branches. He who abides in me, and I in him, he it is that bears much fruit, for apart from me you can do nothing. If a man does not abide in me, he is cast forth as a branch and withers; and the branches are gathered, thrown into the fire and burned. If you abide in me, and my words abide in you, ask whatever you will, and it shall be done for you. By this my Father is glorified, that you bear much fruit, and so prove to be my disciples.*
>
> *—John 15:4-8 RSV*

✓ What is the relationship between a vine and its branches?

✓ How does the relationship between the vine and branch affect fruitfulness?

✓ What does this passage teach about your relationship with Jesus?

✓ Do you want to have a fruitful life? According to this passage what must you do to accomplish this objective?

Points to Remember

To develop a successful lifetime habit of a Quiet Time you need to:

1. Develop competent skills.

2. Know that you have an enemy who will try to stop you.

3. Keep yourself in an environment of accountability for your Quiet Time.

4. Fruitfulness grows out of our intimacy and connectedness to Christ. If we stay closely connected, drawing our sustenance from Him, we will bear fruit. This glorifies God. If we don't stay closely connected, we don't bear fruit. It's that simple!

EVERY MAN A WARRIOR

ASSIGNMENT FOR NEXT WEEK

1. Try to have three to four recorded Quiet Times this week. Be prepared to share some of your best Quiet Time thoughts with the group. Use one to two additional Quiet Times to complete the lesson.

2. Pull out your *EMAW Verse Pack* and place Matthew 22:36-38 in the front window. Memorize the verse this week, saying the reference before and after each time you speak the verse. Next week we will study *A Man of the Word* and start you on your second set of skills.

If you lose your EMAW Verse Pack you can purchase additional copies of the vinyl holder and Scripture memory verses from the website: *www.EveryManAWarrior.com.*

LESSON 4
A MAN
OF THE WORD

NOTE TO LEADERS

It is important to follow the Leader's Guide while leading the lesson. While some items are the same each week, others are specific, one-time instructions that will negatively impact the study if missed. These items are marked with a star. ★

A MAN OF THE WORD

✓ Open the session with prayer.

★✓ Go around the room asking each man to share from one of his Quiet Times. Try to use the *How to Share Your Quiet Time* format described on page 35.

★✓ Ask the men how they did on memorizing their first verse. Ask who would like to try and recite the verse. You may want to go first to get the ball rolling. Eventually you will ask each man to give it a try and recite the verse.

★✓ Remind them to say the reference before and after the verse.

✓ Begin reading the lesson paragraph by paragraph. *A ✓ in front of it means there is a question to discuss.* Stop at each ✓ and ask the questions.

✓ Pages 47-51: Ask each of the questions on these pages. Depending on time, have two to four people give their answer. Try to include everyone.

✓ Pages 49-50: Read *Skills to Help You Memorize Scripture for a Lifetime.* Ask for questions or comments.

✓ Page 50: Have someone read each verse. Depending on time, let as many men as possible share their thoughts on *Being a Man of the Word.*

✓ Page 50: Have each man read his *Why I Want to Be a Man of the Word* paragraph.

✓ Page 52: Read the *Points to Remember* and the *Assignment*.
✓ Place the next verse 2 Timothy 3:16-17 in the front window of your *EMAW Verse Pack* and begin to memorize it this week.
✓ Page 52: Read the *Special Note*.
✓ End in prayer.

EVERY MAN A WARRIOR

A MAN OF THE WORD

My friend Tom asked me to kick off a Discipleship Bible Study with about twenty-five men from his church. They were good guys, ready to grow and wanting to learn. As I started my message, I asked this simple question, *"How many of you have children and want them to grow up to follow the Lord?"* There was immediately 100 percent buy-in; they all raised their hands in agreement.

I gave them a second question. *"How many of you are willing to sacrifice for your children and do the work necessary to build this godly character into their lives?"* Again every hand enthusiastically shot into the air.

Last question; *"How many of you know three verses from the Scripture on raising children?"* There was a hush in the room, and not one hand went up.

In Matthew 22, the Pharisees were trying to trick Jesus and came to Him with a thorny theological question. His answer stunned them—and it scares me. *"You are in error because you do not know the Scriptures"* (Matthew 22:29). Is this true? You and I are in error, you and I mess up, you and I make bad decisions and wonder what happened, all because *we do not know the Scriptures.*

Unfortunately, as men, our errors, wrong thinking, and bad decisions affect those around us, the ones we love the most. Our wrong internal programming gets passed down to the next generation unless we can discover the truth and correct the error.

A pastor and I were discussing the problem of fathers who were not leading in the family and children who were raised in church, yet later in college rejected its truth. He was bemoaning the fact that our culture, advertising, television, and educational systems have become secular and thus were corrupting our families and undermining the teaching of the church.

But is that the real reason? Culture has been anti-Christian for 2,000 years. The darkness is just being dark. The real question is, *"Why is the light of the truth of the Scripture not significantly piercing the darkness of our culture through the people of God?"* Could it be that a major portion of the problem is that we as men *"do not know the Scriptures"?*

✓ Why do you think the light of biblical truth is not more significantly impacting our culture? Jot down at least two ideas or thoughts.

A church that supports my ministry has me preach once a year when the pastor is on vacation. One year I had an exceptionally funny anecdote. The congregation really laughed.

The following year I was greeted by an usher in the church who remarked how he still got a chuckle from that story and repeated it back to me. As we talked further it became shockingly clear that the joke was the only thing he remembered from my sermon.

The vast majority of teaching takes place in our churches in a lecture format. *It's unfortunate that this teaching method carries with it one of the lowest retention rates.*

✓ Review the Learning Pyramid on page 48. How do different teaching methods affect your ability to grow as a Christian? Which method do you most use?

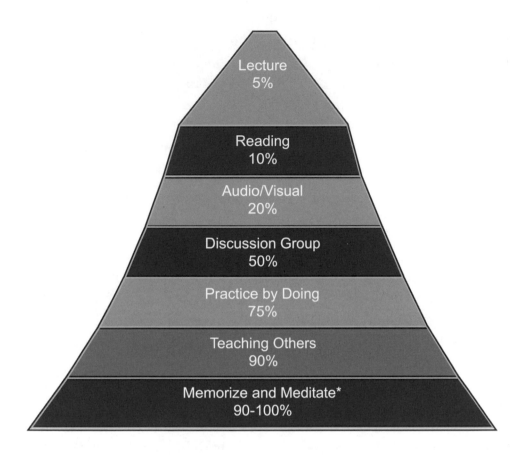

THE LEARNING PYRAMID

The Average Retention Rate of Different Teaching Methods

Adapted from NTL Institute, used by permission. Memorize & Meditate added by the author.

Discipleship is different from a lecture-only format. The learning methods and retention rates used are: memorize and meditate—90 to 100 percent, practice by doing your skills—75 percent, discussing with your group—50 percent, and if you lead an *EVERY MAN A WARRIOR* group (teaching others)—90 percent.

Learning the skill of effectively memorizing and meditating on Scripture is essential to you becoming a man of the Word! *Being a man of the Word is the second building block of discipleship.* See page 20.

A man who stays in the Word becomes equipped for walking with God, raising children, staying married, managing money, going through hard times, enjoying his work, staying morally pure, and making his life count for something eternal. In fact, in 2 Timothy 3:16-17, Paul promises that men will *"be thoroughly equipped for every good work."*

> **All Scripture is God-breathed and is useful for teaching, rebuking, correcting and training in righteousness, so that the man of God may be thoroughly equipped for every good work.**
> —*2 Timothy 3:16-17*

✓ What would it mean for you to be "thoroughly equipped for every good work"?

Starting a New Lifelong Habit— Memorizing and Meditating on Scripture

If we are going to learn a new lifelong skill, we need to get the technique right. A few years ago I joined a gym for the first time. In fact, I hired a trainer for three sessions to get me started correctly. He showed me the correct way to stand when lifting weights. He explained the machines and how they worked different muscles and, most importantly, how not to hurt myself. Then he stood by, watching, encouraging, and correcting me as I learned the routine. It was the best money I could spend. I wanted to start a new lifelong habit and I wanted to get the skills right.

Skills to Help You Memorize Scripture for a Lifetime

1. Have a Quiet Time on the new verse we are memorizing each week. Reread the verse a couple of times and jot down why this verse is important. I normally spend one whole Quiet Time on each new memory verse. That way the verse is already half learned.

2. Always say the reference before and after quoting the verse. The reference is the hardest part to remember. Saying it twice helps it stay connected to the verse.

3. Practice saying the reference and the first phrase of the verse together. This will help in getting the verse started. Then add the next phrase. Keep adding phrases till you have the whole verse. Say the verse out loud whenever possible. Strive to say the verse word perfect.

4. After you have learned the verse, try to review it a couple of times daily. *If you review a learned verse daily for seven weeks it will stay with you for life.*

A MAN OF THE WORD BIBLE STUDY

✓ Study the following verses. Jot down what each says about being a man of the Word.

Colossians 3:16

2 Timothy 2:15

John 8:31-32

Romans 15:4

✓ After studying the above passages and reviewing the thoughts from the reading portion of the study (pages 46-49), write a paragraph titled, *Why I Want to Be a Man of the Word.* Be prepared to share your paragraph with the group.

God gave us the Scripture to give us answers. It is the instruction manual on how to live life successfully. We don't need to mess up our own lives and hurt the ones around us because we don't know the truth.

As I mentioned in the introduction, this course is about skills. *In fact the objective is to help you develop the skills necessary to walk with God for a lifetime.*

Some people fear that Scripture memory is hard! That's a tactic of the Enemy to defeat you before you even start. But let's get some perspective. When the doctors discover your wife has cancer, that's hard. When you walk with your children through wrong choices they have made, that's hard. When you are unemployed for months, with very few prospects and carry mounting bills, or when a good friend commits suicide, *that is hard!*

These types of challenges will come. That much is guaranteed. *Being a man of the Word prepares you for these hardships.* In Psalm 119:92, David says it well: *"If your law had not been my delight, I would have perished in my affliction."*

Hardships will come and they will test your mettle as a man. Being a man of the Word is the best way to prepare for these times of trials. Jesus said, *"I have told you these things, so that in me you may have peace. In this world you will have trouble. But take heart! I have overcome the world"* (John 16:33)

Being a man of the Word is the second building block of discipleship.

✓ Do you feel prepared to face the challenges of life that confront you as a man? Why or why not?

✓ How successfully can a man handle hardship if he does not know these truths?

Points to Remember

1. God gave us the Scripture to give us answers. It is the instruction manual on how to live life successfully. *Being a man of the Word is the second building block of discipleship.* If we don't know the truth, we will mess up our own lives and hurt the ones around us.

2. Different teaching and learning methods greatly affect our retention. Developing your skills in memorizing and meditating on the Word will ensure that you can retain these truths most effectively.

EVERY MAN A WARRIOR

ASSIGNMENT FOR NEXT WEEK

1. Try to record three to four Quiet Times this week. Be prepared to share some of your best Quiet Time thoughts with the group. Use one or two additional Quiet Times to complete the lesson or spend the time meditating and memorizing your current verses.

2. Place 2 Timothy 3:16-17 in the front window of your *EMAW Verse Pack* and begin to memorize it this week.

3. Be ready to recite from memory your two verses at the beginning of next week's lesson.

Special Note

Most of the verses used in this course are from the New International Version (NIV), the most widely used Bible translation in the U.S. I have taken a few verses from other versions because the translation is more accurate. If you lose your verse pack, you can purchase a vinyl pack and printed verses from the website *www.EveryManAWarrior.com.*

We will all memorize in the same version because it is very confusing to hear people quoting different versions. Then we will all be on the same page and more able to encourage each other in Scripture memory. It is perfectly okay to have your Quiet Time and Bible reading in another version.

Leader's Guide to

LESSON 5

MEDITATION: THINKING WITH PURPOSE

NOTE TO LEADERS

This lesson has some special items marked with a star. ★

MEDITATION: THINKING WITH PURPOSE

★✓ Break into pairs and recite your verses to each other. Have one man hold the cards and say the reference while the other quotes the verse and also says the reference at the end of the verse.

★✓ Introduce the men to the *Completion Record* at the back of the book. *If anyone has said the verses word-perfect,* let him have someone else initial and date the first line. Sign off on any of the completion record that applies. Read the *Course Requirements for Completion* at the end of the completion record.

- Finish all nine lessons.
- Memorize and quote six Scripture passages.
- Record twenty Quiet Times or more.

✓ Open the session with prayer.

★✓ Ask the participants how they are doing with memorizing verses. Are they saying the reference *before* and *after?* Are they saying the reference and first phrase together?

★✓ Reread *Skills to Help You Memorize Scripture* on pages 49-50 .

✓ Go around the room, asking each man to share one Quiet Time. Turn to the Scripture where he is reading.

✓ Page 54: Ask someone to start reading the lesson and go around the circle, each man reading a paragraph or two.

✓ Page 55–59: Ask each of the questions on these pages. Depending on time, have two to four people give their answer. Try to include everyone.

✓ Pages 58-59: Read the *Points to Remember* and the *Assignment*.

✓ Page 59: Place Joshua 1:8 in the front window of your *EMAW Verse Pack* and begin to memorize it this week.

✓ End in prayer. As leader, pray for the men to become *men of the Word.*

MEDITATION: THINKING WITH PURPOSE

I met Dr. Dave when we had just moved to Omaha. I needed a checkup, and his office was located down the street. As we chatted about family and what I did, I mentioned how I helped men grow in their relationship with Christ. This brought an inquisitive smile, and he explained how he had recently been to a Promise Keepers conference and had dedicated his life to Christ.

As a disciple-maker, you cannot let these opportunities go! I said, "That's fantastic! Has anyone shown you how to have a Quiet Time?" He said, "No, what's that?" I explained it was a time of reading the Bible and talking to Jesus about our lives, so that we can grow as Christians. "Would you like to learn how?" He said, "Yes!"

That started a four-year journey when Dr. Dave spent his one free morning each week with me for two hours in the discipleship process. Somewhere about year two, he began to lead people to Christ. First, it was his office manager and then a patient named Alan.

Dr. Dave and I continued to meet, and he started discipling Alan. They started having Quiet Times and for the first year things went great. But then Alan bought a fixer-upper fourplex apartment building and it began to consume all of his time. He'd leave work at 5:30 and spend until midnight working on his new project.

Without meditation, the Scripture tends to stay cerebral, rather than actually touching your heart and changing your life.

One morning when Dr. Dave and Alan were meeting, Alan confessed, *"I'm tired, I don't have my lesson done, I haven't been having my Quiet Times, I never see my kids, and my wife is mad too."*

Dave smiled knowingly and said, "Let's look at the verse that God gave me yesterday in my Quiet Time when I was thinking of you." They turned to Proverbs 23:4. *"Do not wear yourself out to get rich; have the wisdom to show restraint."* Alan was convicted. That night after work he went home, hugged his wife, played with his kids, and started his next day with an extra long Quiet Time.

I have seen this happen hundreds of times—God speaks to men in a Quiet Time as they meditate on the Scripture. Our new verse, 2 Timothy 3:16-17, says the Word is meant to teach us—and sometimes rebuke us. It trains us in righteousness, which means "right-wise living and thinking." Developing our skills in meditating on the Word will equip us for whatever challenges we face.

Meditation is the art of "thinking with purpose." *Without meditation, the Scripture tends to stay cerebral, rather than actually touching your heart and changing your life.* In this lesson we will sharpen our skills in meditation. Your Quiet Time Journal has the methods listed to remind you to keep developing this skill. Keep practicing these meditation methods in your Quiet Time. *When you have developed good meditation skills, your Quiet Time will give you greater insight into the Scripture.*

✓ Meditate on the following verses using the Ask Questions method. Ask yourself which meditation question best reveals the truth of the verse. Some verses will have more than one. See example below:

Something new about God This is the message we have heard from him and declare to you: God is light; in him there is no darkness at all. (1 John 1:5)

_____I will instruct you and teach you in the way you should go; I will counsel you and watch over you. (Psalms 32:8)

_____Do not merely listen to the word, and so deceive yourselves. Do what it says. (James 1:22)

_____For where you have envy and selfish ambition, there you find disorder and every evil practice. (James 3:16)

Ask Questions

Is there:

A command to obey

A promise to claim

A sin to avoid

An application to make

Something new about God

Ask: Who, What, When, Where, Why

Emphasize:
Different words

Rewrite:
In your own words

✓ *Emphasizing different words* forces your mind to see the implications of each key word in a verse. Read and reread 2 Timothy 3:16-17 below, giving special emphasis to the *underlined* words. *Accentuate the underlined word* or phrase and jot down two or three thoughts that come to mind as you think about the implications of the emphasized word. Use a thesaurus or dictionary to stimulate your thinking.

All Scripture is God-breathed and is useful for teaching, rebuking, correcting and training in righteousness, so that the man of God may be thoroughly equipped for every good work.

—*2 Timothy 3:16-17, emphasis added*

All

God-breathed

useful

teaching

rebuking

correcting

training

thoroughly equipped

✓ *Rewriting a verse in your own words* will allow you to combine all your meditation in a way that explains the verse. It is meant to increase the understanding of what the verse means to you. Rewrite 2 Timothy 3:16-17 in your own words. Use your meditations from the previous exercise to help. Be prepared to share your thoughts.

All Scripture is God-breathed and is useful for teaching, rebuking, correcting and training in righteousness, so that the man of God may be thoroughly equipped for every good work.

—*2 Timothy 3:16-17*

Do not let this Book of the Law depart from your mouth; meditate on it day and night, so that you may be careful to do everything written in it. Then you will be prosperous and successful.

—Joshua 1:8

✓ Meditate on Joshua 1:8 using the Ask Questions method. Circle those that apply and jot down your thoughts.

Ask Questions
Is there:
A command to obey
A promise to claim
A sin to avoid
An application to make
Something new about God
Ask: Who, What, When, Where, Why
Emphasize: Different words
Rewrite: In your own words

✓ Use the *Who, What, When, Where, Why Questions* to meditate on Joshua 1:8. Jot down your thoughts.

Who:

What:

When:

Where:

Why:

✓ How does meditating impact your understanding of the verse?

✓ Rewrite Joshua 1:8 in your own words. Be prepared to share.

✓ How does meditating on the Word affect your ability to *do it or apply it to your life?*

✓ Why is keeping the Word *cerebral* a problem? Why does a verse need to touch our hearts?

Points to Remember

1. Meditation is the art of *"thinking with purpose."*

2. Without meditation the Scripture tends to stay cerebral, rather than touching your heart, stimulating application and changing your life.

3. Developing your skills in meditation will greatly enhance your ability to become a *"man of the Word."*

ASSIGNMENT FOR NEXT WEEK

1. Try to have three or four recorded Quiet Times this week using one or two meditation methods each day. Use additional Quiet Times to complete the lesson and work on your verses.

2. Place Joshua 1:8 in the front window of your *EMAW Verse Pack* and begin to memorize it this week.

3. Review, review, review is the key to Scripture memory. Review your verses at least once a day, every day.

4. Remember, we only retain 10 percent of what we read, so keep a pen in hand to underline, jot notes, or ask questions when reading the lesson. Come with lesson 6 finished and be ready to discuss.

Leader's Guide to

LESSON 6
YOU DO NOT HAVE BECAUSE YOU DO NOT ASK

NOTE TO LEADERS

This lesson has some special items marked with a star. ★

YOU DO NOT HAVE BECAUSE YOU DO NOT ASK

★✓ Break into pairs and recite all your verses to each other. Have one man hold the cards and say the reference while the other quotes the verse and also says the reference at the end of the verse.

✓ Sign off on any of the *Completion Record* that applies in the back of the book.

✓ Open the session with prayer.

★✓ Check on their progress with memorizing verses. Remind the men that review, review, review is the key. Try to review your verses every day.

★✓ Remind them to do at least one Quiet Time on the new verse each week doing all of the meditation exercises. Then the verse is half-learned.

✓ Go around the room, asking each man to share one Quiet Time.

✓ Begin reading the lesson paragraph by paragraph.

✓ Pages 64-67: Ask each of the questions on these pages. Depending on time, have two to four people give their answer. Try to include everyone. Look up and read each verse together.

✓ Page 66: Have each person read his summary on prayer.

✓ Page 66-67: Depending on time, have as many as possible

share their Ask Questions meditations and their *rewrite* of John 16:24.

✓ Page 67: Read the *Points to Remember.*

✓ Page 67-68: Read the *Special Note* together. Discuss how you can help each other be successful in building the spiritual habits of Quiet Time and Scripture memory.

✓ Page 68: Read the *Assignment.* Place John 16:24 in the front window of your *EMAW Verse Pack* and memorize it this week.

✓ End in prayer.

Time to order your next book. Go to *www.EveryManAWarrior.com* to order your next book in the EVERY MAN A WARRIOR series. Groups with married men should order *Book 2–Marriage and Raising Children.* Groups with single men may want to jump to *Book 3–Money, Sex, Work, Hard Times, and Making your Life Count.*

YOU DO NOT HAVE BECAUSE YOU DO NOT ASK

Scott and Joyce had been married just a year and were struggling. Joyce longed for a piano. In fact, soon after they were married, Joyce had asked for one. But Scott, an independent contractor, said they just couldn't afford it. Work had been slow, and in the jobs he bid and contracted, he had not always made as much income as he had hoped. Joyce kept struggling with her desire for a piano. Each month she would bring it up, and the subsequent arguments were more and more agonizing.

Scott and Joyce were saving to buy a house, plus paying off his college loans. They budgeted their income, tithed regularly, and were trying to live by godly priorities. They both worked but had little left at the end of each month. Scott and Joyce also came from families with different income levels. Scott came from a farm family and worked his way through college, whereas Joyce's dad, an executive with a major insurance company, had a huge salary.

Joyce saw the $7,000 they had in savings and felt surely they could spend some of that for her piano. But Scott had scrimped and sacrificed before marriage to start his business and put together a down payment for a house. He wasn't willing to sacrifice his hard work on a piano, something he felt was a luxury item. So the discussions would always end with his words, *"We just can't afford it."*

During a short vacation to visit Joyce's family, Scott decided to have an extra long Quiet Time, reading the Bible in the upstairs bedroom. Joyce was downstairs playing the family piano and having the time of her life. Scott liked hearing her play. He had not realized how much she enjoyed it. *Maybe I should spend the house savings and buy her a piano. It would be a nice gesture and would end these fights,* Scott thought. But God had something else in mind.

While Scott was reading and meditating, a part of James 4:2 seemed to leap from the page. *"You do not have because you do not ask God."* Well, that's not true, Scott thought. If I had just made the amount of money I had hoped for on some jobs we could have bought a piano. Scott read the verse again, *"You do not have because you do not ask God."* It was cross-referenced to John 16:24: *"Until now you have not asked for anything in my name. Ask and you will receive, and your joy will be complete!"*

Scott remembered a time in college when he had first become a Christian. He was broke, and when he prayed for the finances to go to a Christian conference, God had sent him money from a friend. The friend had written a note saying, *"I don't know why, but God told me to send you this money in my Quiet Time."* It had been the exact amount Scott needed. Would prayer still work? Scott decided to give it a try.

Over the next two months Scott secretly prayed daily that God would provide his wife with a piano. He prayed for a nice one that she would really enjoy. In about two weeks the miracle began to happen. A college friend stopped by and paid off an old loan that Scott had long forgotten about. $200! Joyce thought it strange when Scott suggested they put it away as seed money for a piano. An older Christian couple took them to dinner and gave them $200 just because they felt a prompting from the Lord. Joyce began to get suspicious when Scott decided to put that money in the piano envelope too. So Scott told her of his prayer adventure with God. They both started praying.

A month later Joyce got some money as a birthday gift and Scott got a bonus for finishing a job over the weekend. $850 was now sitting in their piano envelope in just three months! Scott and Joyce were ecstatic.

One Saturday afternoon they started looking at pianos. Their hearts sank. The lower-priced used pianos at the local store were fifteen to twenty years old, looked shabby, and were priced at $1800. The salesman said they could finance the rest, but that didn't seem right if James 4:2 was really true. Scott and Joyce went home discouraged.

The next day after church, Scott was browsing through the want ads when he came across "Piano for Sale - Moving, $850." Still discouraged, Scott thought, *That must be a piece of junk after what we saw at the store.* At that moment he felt a jolt in his spirit as if to say, *"You call on this one."* So Scott called. The piano was only six years old. An Air Force family had bought it new for their daughter. She had taken lessons, but lost interest after two years. The family just didn't want to move it.

Scott said they'd be right down. It was beautiful. Joyce loved it. The piano had hardly been played. They were the first to come look, cash in hand. God had given them a piano!

✓ What stands out to you about prayer from Scott and Joyce's story?

✓ What answers to prayer have you received?

✓ Why do you think Scott waited so long to pray about this issue?

✓ Is there any issue that you are currently struggling with that you have not prayed about?

✓ What do these verses teach us about prayer?

Matthew 7:7-11

Luke 18:1

✓ What are some of the benefits of prayer?

Psalms 62:8

Psalms 34:4

Philippians 4:6-7

✓ What are some conditions for answered prayer?

1 John 5:14-15

Psalms 66:18-20

James 4:3

John 15:7

✓ Write a summary of what you have learned about prayer from the above study. Be prepared to share it with the group.

Until now you have not asked for anything in my name. Ask and you will receive, and your joy will be complete.
—John 16:24

Ask Questions

Is there:

A command to obey

A promise to claim

A sin to avoid

An application to make

Something new about God

Ask: Who, What, When, Where, Why

Emphasize:
Different words

Rewrite:
In your own words

✓ Meditate on John 16:24 using the Ask Questions method. Jot down your thoughts.

✓ Rewrite John 16:24 in your own words. Be prepared to share with the group.

Points to Remember

1. God loves you and delights in giving His children good things if they will just ask. If we don't ask, we miss out.

2. There are conditions for answered prayer. As our heavenly Father, God won't give us something that is not good for us.

3. Prayer is more than just obtaining things. As we grow in prayer, we will discover that peace, joy, and fellowship with our heavenly Father are some of its greatest benefits.

Special Note

Some of you may have joined this study because you wanted to study about Money, Marriage, Raising Children, or the other topics in Books Two and Three. Right now it is important to develop your skills in meditating on the Word through your Quiet Time and Scripture Memory. If these skills are not in place first, you will be limited in your ability to study and apply these other topics.

Some groups gradually drop the Scripture Memory verses or the Quiet Time part of the study because it seems too hard or takes too much effort. *This is the worst thing you can do if you want to grow spiritually and see your life change.*

Spiritual growth does not occur by just attending religious activities or by strengthening your determination to better manage your behavior. True spiritual growth only happens as God changes you on the inside. Your time meditating on the Scripture when you have a Quiet Time or working on memorizing verses are the fastest and most effective ways for this transformation to take place.

So don't cheat yourself. Do the work like you promised in signing the commitment on page 22. Spend one whole Quiet Time reviewing old verses plus meditating and working on your new verse each week. Also try to review all your verses every day. Some men do this over lunch or before they go to bed.

The groups that drop the Scripture Memory or Quiet Times lose 70 to 80 percent of the transforming power of discipleship.

EVERY MAN A WARRIOR

ASSIGNMENT FOR NEXT WEEK

1. Try to record three to four Quiet Times this week. Use additional Quiet Times to complete the lesson or spend time working on your verses.

2. Place John 16:24 in the front window of your *EMAW Verse Pack* and memorize it this week. Be prepared to review all your verses with another person.

3. Order your next book by going to *www.EveryManAWarrior.com.*

Leader's Guide to

THE REAL PURPOSE OF PRAYER

NOTE TO LEADERS

This lesson has some special items marked with a star. ★

THE REAL PURPOSE OF PRAYER

✓ Break into pairs and recite all your verses to each other. Have one man hold the cards and say the reference while the other quotes the verse and repeats the reference at the end of the verse.

✓ Open the session with prayer.

★✓ Ask the men to count up the number of recorded Quiet Times. Does any man have more than ten? Fifteen? Sign off on the *Completion Record* in the back of the book. Cheer those who have done well; encourage those who have struggled.

✓ Go around the room, asking each man to share one Quiet Time.

✓ Begin reading the lesson paragraph by paragraph.

✓ Page 71-78: Ask each of the questions on these pages. Depending on time, have two to four people give their answer. Try to include everyone.

✓ Page 77: Read the *Points to Remember.*

✓ Pages 77-78: Read the *Assignment.* Place Philippians 4:6-7 in the front window of your *EMAW Verse Pack* and memorize it this week.

✓ Page 78: Practice the *WAR* method of prayer as a group. Ask the group to turn to page 75. Follow the instructions on page 70.

★ ✓ *Leader:* Be sure to read the following instructions to the group for the WAR prayer exercise. Have everyone turn to page 75.

• We will each pray three times using the format on page 75. I will start with the *Praise and Thanksgiving* form of prayer. Then we will go around the room and *each of you will pray a similar praise or thanksgiving, using the illustration as a guide.*

• After everyone has prayed, I will start the Admit form of prayer, and we will pray around again.

• After everyone has prayed, I will start the Request form of prayer, and we will pray around again. Then I will close.

THE REAL PURPOSE OF PRAYER

EVERY MAN A WARRIOR

Rodney was a brand new Christian. We had been meeting for only five weeks. Since he didn't grow up in church, the Christian life was completely new to him. But he was excited about Quiet Times and had three verses memorized.

Up until that fifth week, I had been the only one to pray in our sessions. But now we were studying the chapter on prayer. I knew it might be uncomfortable for him to pray, so I tried to take some of the pressure off. After our lesson on prayer I said, *"Let's both pray this time. I'll start and you can close."* I said a short prayer and then nodded to him since I knew he still had his eyes open. Rodney started out really well for not having prayed before and talked to the Lord from his heart. When it was time to stop praying he didn't quite know how, so he paused for a second. Then with finality he said, *"That's all, Lord, over and out!"*

What is prayer? In the ABCs of Quiet Time, the C is communicating back to the Lord what we feel he has shown us. That's a good place to start. In lesson 7 we will begin to expand our prayer time and our understanding of prayer. Our prayer acronym is WAR, which stands for Worship, Admit, and Request.

Worship should be a fundamental focus of our relationship with God. As you spend time with God in the Word, prayer, and worship, you will begin to perceive His love for you. He values you highly, longs to spend time with you, and never tires of hearing you pray.

In my early years as a Christian, I felt that I should express my love for God by all the work and ministry I was doing for Him. We easily fall into this trap. It took years to learn that what God really wanted, first and foremost, was to spend time with me. I think the letter below describes what the Lord wants to communicate to you and me.

A Letter from God

My son,

Do you not know how much I love you? Do not be deceived and do not be afraid, because I will never stop loving you. You are my son! I am working in your life because you are my son. Come to me. Cry out to me. I love to hear you pray. I created you so that we could walk together and talk together often. I reward those who earnestly seek me.

You are my son. I love you as one of my children. Nothing can change that. Do not fear and do not be afraid. All your sins have been forgiven and they are swept from my sight. Nothing you do will ever change how much I love you.

God

✓ What are your thoughts about *A Letter from God?*

✓ How does God loving you, no matter what, influence your relationship with Him?

✓ What do you think of the statement: *"Worship should be a fundamental focus of our relationship with God"?*

✓ How does worship affect your ability to perceive and receive God's love?

How We Grow in Prayer

I came to Christ my freshman year of college. In those early days of my walk with the Lord, prayer was mostly about getting things from God. One of my first Christian conferences was titled, *God Can Make It Happen!* The speaker told story after story of how God had, through prayer, supernaturally intervened in his life to meet needs or provide some miracle. I went away excited to see what I could pray and ask God for.

As we grow and mature, our prayer life should also change.

When my daughters were very young we had a standing weekly father-daughter time. We drove a few blocks to the local McDonald's for a Happy Meal. At that age it was all they wanted, to be with Dad and have a Happy Meal.

As they got older their desires and requests changed. During their teenage years they asked for clothes, computers, a prom dress, and then a car. Now that they are both adults, they call home for other reasons. Recently their questions have been more about life partners, careers, and managing money.

My daughters no longer ask for a Happy Meal. Now they just need to talk, to share their hearts, their struggles, fears, or joys. Sometimes they even ask what I think.

It's similar with God and prayer. In our early years as Christians, our prayers are mostly about asking God for stuff. And that's okay. He's trying to teach us that we can really trust Him and that His promises are true. But as we grow and mature, our prayer life should also change.

We should always tell God our needs. But some Christians are caught in a permanent spiritual adolescence. They keep asking God for trinkets, like He is some kind of spiritual Santa Claus, and they miss the joys of a more spiritually adult relationship.

✓ What are your thoughts from *How We Grow in Prayer?*

Worshipping Prayer: PTL Method— Praise, Thank, Listen

Worshipping prayer is about **praising** God for who He is and who He is becoming to you. Prayer is also about sitting in the presence of God to pour out your heart to Him. I used to think that prayer was just about me. But when you and I talk to the Lord, when we pour out our hearts to God, it is actually about Him as well. As a father He longs for our fellowship and never tires of hearing about our fears, joys, struggles, or desires.

Worshipping prayer is also about **thanking** Him for what He has done in your life. Whenever I am feeling discouraged, I spend some time thanking the Lord, recounting all that He has blessed me with. The cloud usually lifts. "He who brings thanksgiving as his sacrifice honors me" (Psalms 50:23 RSV).

It took me a long time to learn that prayer is also about **listening**. Hearing from God in our Quiet Time is an important part of making good decisions. For most of us God speaks through His Word. You may have already seen God speak to your heart on an issue as you were reading the Scripture.

But God also speaks to our hearts through the still, quiet voice of the Holy Spirit. If what you hear lines up with the Scripture, jot down the thought and try to get godly counsel from a mature Christian on this decision. If what you heard is from the Lord, it will be confirmed over time.

Communication with God – WAR Exercise

Worship in Prayer—PTL

1. *Praise* Him for who He is and what He has done.
2. *Thank* Him for His blessings, and the privilege of calling Him Father.
3. *Listen* to Him. Check what you hear against the Scripture, and wait patiently for Him to confirm it over time.

ADMIT—This is the confession of sin and asking for His forgiveness.

REQUEST—My needs: wisdom, help, finances, children, wife, other relationships, work, right attitudes, morally pure thoughts, and so on.

✓ Read the *WAR* examples of prayer on page 75. Try to practice them in your Quiet Time. Let them give you a place to start as you learn to talk as a son to your heavenly father, the God of the universe.

We will begin to pray out loud together as a group at the end of this session. If this is the first time for you to pray out loud in a group, relax. You can use the exact words of the examples above or just pray a few words like you were talking to a friend. Over time, you will feel more comfortable praying with others. Praying as a group can become a kind of spiritual "super-glue" that bonds the lives of men together.

WAR PRAYING EXAMPLES

Worship in Prayer—Praise, Thank, Listen.

I love You, Jesus. I give You praise, glory, and honor. I praise You for who You are and I thank You for Your goodness to me.
I praise You that You died for me and chose me to be one of Your sons.
I thank You for Your blessings. Thank You that You have been faithful to me.
I worship You, Jesus. I praise You. You are God.
It is my privilege to know You. Thank You for the joy of walking with You.
Lord, is there anything that You want to say to me? I'm listening.

Admit—The confession of sin and asking for God's forgiveness.

Lord, I admit that I've really struggled and I ask Your forgiveness for_____.
Forgive me for my attitudes toward or about _____.
Lord, forgive me that I have been so angry over _____
_____.
I ask Your forgiveness for lust, pride, arrogance, unforgiveness against _____.

Request—Bringing my needs before the Lord.

Lord, I pray for my wife and ask _____.
Lord, I pray for my children and ask _____.
Give me wisdom, Lord, as I _____.
Jesus, I pray for my needs (others' needs) in the area of _____
_____.
I pray for the people around me who do not know Christ. I pray for
_____.

Do not be anxious about anything, but in everything, by prayer and petition, with thanksgiving, present your requests to God. And the peace of God, which transcends all understanding, will guard your hearts and your minds in Christ Jesus.

—*Philippians 4:6-7*

✓ Meditate on Philippians 4:6-7, the passage above, using the Ask Questions method of meditation. Jot down your observations.

✓ Use the Who, What, When, Where, Why questions to stimulate your thinking. Jot down your thoughts.

Now *Emphasize Different Words* in Philippians 4:6-7. Use a dictionary or thesaurus to expand your understanding of the words.

Do not be
anything
everything
prayer and petition
thanksgiving
peace of God
transcends
guard your hearts

Ask Questions

Is there:

A command to obey

A promise to claim

A sin to avoid

An application to make

Something new about God

Ask: Who, What, When, Where, Why

Emphasize:
Different words

Rewrite:
In your own words

✓ Now rewrite Philippians 4:6-7 in your own words. Use your thoughts from page 76.

Points to Remember

1. Whether you have been a praying Christian for many years or you are just learning about prayer, your time talking to God can become some of your most cherished and joyful moments in life.

2. God wants us to unburden ourselves of every anxiety, fear, and need. He wants to carry these burdens for you, answer your prayers, and give you His peace.

3. As we grow in maturity, our prayer life will also mature. Worshipping God and praying for others will become a higher priority than just "getting things" from God.

EVERY MAN A WARRIOR

ASSIGNMENT FOR NEXT WEEK

1. Try to record three to four Quiet Times this week. Use additional Quiet Times to do the lesson and spend time working on your verses.

2. If your current place and time are not working, take action now. Change your time and place for Quiet Time.

3. Practice the *WAR* method of prayer in your Quiet Time this week. Begin praying for the men in your group to have consistent and quality times with the Lord. Pray against the Enemy attacking the Quiet Times of the men in the group.

4. Place Philippians 4:6-7 in the front window of your *EMAW Verse Pack* and memorize it this week.

5. *"That's all, over and out!"*

✓ End the session by turning back to page 75 and practice using the WAR format of prayer as a group. (Leader: your instructions are in the Leader's Guide box on page 70.)

Leader's Guide to

LESSON 8
THE SECRET TO A CHANGED LIFE

NOTE TO LEADERS

You can download the Leader's Guide from the website *www.EveryManAWarrior.com* to make it easier to follow while leading the lesson.

THE SECRET TO A CHANGED LIFE

✓ Break into pairs and recite your verses to each other.

✓ Sign off on the *Completion Record.*

✓ Open the session with prayer.

✓ Ask each man to share one Quiet Time.

✓ Begin reading the lesson paragraph by paragraph.

✓ Pages 82–85: Ask each of the questions on these pages. Depending on time, have two to four people give their answer. Try to include everyone.

✓ Page 83: Luke 6:46-49 *Note to leader:* The key teaching of this passage is the difference between those who apply the Word and those who don't.

✓ Page 84 *Special note:* What do you think of our new goal for Scripture memory?

✓ Page 85: Go through all the memorized verses and share what possible application they could make from these verses.

✓ Pages 85- 86: Read the *Points to Remember* and the *Assignment.*

✓ Page 86: Place James 1:22 in the front window of your *EMAW Verse Pack* and memorize it this week.

✓ Page 86: End in group prayer using the *WAR* method. Follow the pattern outlined on page 75 and the Leader's Guide instructions on page 70.

THE SECRET TO A CHANGED LIFE

I was having breakfast with Kent, a pastor in our area. He started his church with a few families just ten years ago. Now more than 600 people attended. He had two additional pastors and a competent administrative staff, but he was frustrated by the lack of mature spiritual leaders available to run the ministries of the church. He was tired and overwhelmed with the demands of his position as senior pastor.

I began to ask questions and zeroed in on these points: What was he doing to build men spiritually, and how effectively was the leadership training men to do the work of ministry?

To my surprise, he felt that they were doing an adequate job. So I probed deeper. What percentage of the people in the church were having a daily Quiet Time? What percentage of the people in the church knew how to share their faith and were successfully leading people to Christ? To each question, he used the same words, *"I don't know, but I think most of them."* I knew that was probably not the case.

In another situation, Barry and Selma were referred to me by a friend from our church. They were deeply in debt. They both worked but had a large mortgage on their beautiful home. They enjoyed their boat, which they had bought along with a lakefront second home—and second mortgage. They tried to take at least one overseas vacation each year and sometimes a winter cruise. Their cars were both new but on payments.

They came to me because they were about to be foreclosed on. Creditors were constantly calling. When I asked what they felt needed to change, they both became angry and said, *"Well, whatever we do, we're not going to lower our standard of living!"*

These two scenarios each have a common theme: *the amazing capacity for humans to live in denial.*

George Barna wrote a book in 1990 called *The Frog in the Kettle* (Ventura, CA: Gospel Light Publishing, 1990). It described how subtle cultural changes over time had radically transformed our society for the worse. He described how the church had changed as well—and statistically was no different from much of the unchurched.

While revival is breaking out in other parts of the world, the number of Christians in America has remained unchanged since the 1950s.

Developing your love relationship with God causes you to want to obey Him.

What are we doing wrong? The Christian life is not supposed to be powerless. As we learned from the Learning Pyramid in lesson 4, a lecture-style format in teaching and preaching has a very low retention rate. However, the greatest tragedy is not that people only remember 5 percent of their pastor's sermon—*but that most Christians fail to apply any of what they have heard and their lives remain unchanged.*

James 1:22 warns of this deception. Before we start studying the practical areas of money, marriage, raising children, work, purity, and hard times, we must grasp the most fundamental reason to study the Scripture: *to do what it says.*

Do not merely listen to the word, and so deceive yourselves. Do what it says.

—James 1:22

In lesson 1 we discovered that the *One Thing* in the Christian life is to develop our love relationship with God. Hopefully by now your Christian life has changed. If you have been growing in your Quiet Times, you may have already discovered this discipleship mystery: *Developing your love relationship with God causes you to want to obey Him.* Nobody wants to disappoint someone they love deeply. It's one of the biggest secrets of why discipleship works and transforms a person's life.

Whoever has my commands and obeys them, he is the one who loves me. He who loves me will be loved by my Father, and I too will love him and show myself to him.

— John 14:21

✓ Meditate on John 14:21 and record your thoughts. What happens in your relationship with God when you obey Him?

✓ What is the connection between your love relationship with God and your ability to obey His commands?

✓ Do you agree that developing your relationship with God causes you to want to obey Him? Why or why not?

✓ What do you think of the old adage, *"Rules without relationship leads to rebellion?"* How does this apply to your Christianity?

✓ What other truth about obeying God's commands is found in 1 John 5:3?

✓ Meditate on James 1:22 using the Ask Questions method. Jot your observations below.

Do not merely listen to the word, and so deceive yourselves. Do what it says.

—James 1:22

✓ Meditate on James 1:22 using the *Emphasize Different Words* method and record your thoughts.

> **Ask Questions**
>
> **Is there:**
>
> A command to obey
>
> A promise to claim
>
> A sin to avoid
>
> An application to make
>
> Something new about God
>
> Ask: Who, What, When, Where, Why
>
> **Emphasize:**
> Different words
>
> **Rewrite:**
> In your own words

✓ Read and study Luke 6:46-49. What is the key teaching of this passage? Be prepared to discuss your thoughts with the group.

But the man who looks intently into the perfect law that gives freedom, and continues to do this, not forgetting what he has heard, but doing it—he will be blessed in what he does.

—James 1:25 (emphasis added)

✓ Meditate on James 1:25 using the *Emphasize Different Words* method. Jot down your thoughts below. Use a dictionary or thesaurus to stimulate your thinking.

looks
intently
perfect
gives freedom
continues
not forgetting
but doing it
will be blessed

✓ Now rewrite James 1:25 in your own words, using the thoughts from your meditations above. Be prepared to share your thoughts and rewrite.

Special Note

In lesson 4 we made it our goal to memorize our verses and say them word-perfect. It's a good standard and place to start. *But the real goal and purpose of Scripture memory and meditation is to be able to apply the verse to our lives and to have the Word readily available to share with someone else.*

✓ What do you think of this new goal for Scripture memory?

✓ On page 85 review all your previously memorized verses. You may use one of your Quiet Times to do this page. Jot down *how each verse below could be applied to your life,* or *one truth you could share with someone else.* See the example below. We will discuss your answers as a group.

Application Exercise (Example)

Matthew 22:36-38
For Myself
I need to spend time with Jesus so that I can love God more. I want to have a thirty-minute Quiet Time every day.
For Someone Else
Or: I will encourage my brothers in developing their love relationship with God, by asking them what they are learning in their Quiet Times.

Or: When I witness to my friend at work I want to emphasize that Christianity is not about a set of rules but about being able to have a relationship with a God who loves us.

---

2 Timothy 3:16-17

Joshua 1:8

John 16:24

Philippians 4:6-7

James 1:22

Points to Remember

1. The most fundamental reason to read, study, listen to, memorize, or meditate on the Scripture is *"to do what it says."*

2. When a Christian has a consistent and meaningful Quiet Time and his love for the Lord is growing, he will eagerly obey what the Scripture says. *It is one of the greatest secrets of why discipleship works.*

3. Being able to obey and apply God's Word is the key to a transformed life in Christ. Without obedience and application, our lives end up being unchanged—no different than the rest of the world.

EVERY MAN A WARRIOR

ASSIGNMENT FOR NEXT WEEK

1. Have three to four recorded Quiet Times this week. Be prepared to share.

2. Place James 1:22 in the front window of your *EMAW Verse Pack* and memorize it this week.

3. Our next lesson, *Every Man a Bulldog,* is designed to help you evaluate your own spiritual growth and the health of the group. It is also a week to get caught up if you're behind.

4. Finish any lessons that you have not done.

5. Do the *Proficiency Evaluation* for the course, lessons 1–9, pages 93–95. Try to fill in the answers without looking first. Then go back to find and check your answers.

✓ End the group in prayer using the WAR method. Follow the outline on page 75.

Leader's Guide to

LESSON 9
EVERY MAN A BULLDOG

NOTE TO LEADERS

You can download the Leader's Guide from the website *www.EveryManAWarrior.com* to make it easier to follow while leading the lesson.

EVERY MAN A BULLDOG

✓ Break into pairs and recite all your verses to each other. Sign off on the *Completion Record.*

✓ Ask the men if they have finished all the requirements for Book 1. Encourage them to fulfill requirements to finish.

✓ Open the session with prayer.

✓ Ask each man to share one Quiet Time.

✓ Begin reading the lesson paragraph by paragraph.

✓ Pages 89–91: Discuss the questions concerning being a bulldog and how we grow as Christians. *(Leader: Try to find one thing you can compliment each man on in his efforts so far on EVERY MAN A WARRIOR.)*

✓ Pages 91–92: Read and discuss *Leaders Lead* and *Successful Study Guidelines for EVERY MAN A WARRIOR.* Ask the men how to make the study better.

✓ Pages 93–95 Answer each of the *Proficiency Evaluation* questions. Go around having each man read a question and his answer. Discuss whenever possible.

✓ Pages 95-96: Read Hebrews 12:11 together. Have each man share his meditations and rewrite of the verse.

✓ Pages 96-97: Read the *Points to Remember* and the *Assignment.*

✓ End in group prayer using the *WAR* method. Follow the pattern outlined on page 75 and the Leader's Guide on page 70. During the *Request* section, have the men pray for each other that they would grow into the *Spiritual Bulldogs* God wants them to be.

EVERY MAN A BULLDOG

Some discipleship groups make it. Others do not. Over the years I've noticed an interesting characteristic about the groups that are successful. *They have at least one discipleship bulldog.*

One of the characteristics of a bulldog is that he sinks his teeth into whatever he takes hold of and hangs on. You can try to get it out of his mouth. You can play tug of war. But a bulldog hangs on with jaws of steel. Each group needs at least one or two discipleship bulldogs.

About this time in the discipleship process, men sometimes hit a tough patch. The fascination with discipleship has worn off. Having a daily Quiet Time and keeping up on verses becomes work. The desire to drop these disciplines and spiritually put your feet up is strong.

I was discipling a group of men in western Nebraska. These eight guys were doing great. I saw them only once a month, but each week they paired off and met for the lesson. But the reason this group was a success was because of two of the guys, Brad and Terry. They were bulldogs!

They sunk their teeth into discipleship and hung on. They shared excitedly what the Lord had shown them in their Quiet Times. They not only memorized the required verses but others as well. They got the lesson done and encouraged their brothers to do the same. On Sundays they even asked the other men how their Quiet Times were going and what the Lord was teaching them.

These two guys made the whole group a success by setting the pace. The other six men began to put in more time on their verses and Quiet Times. They wanted to have something to share since Brad and Terry were getting such good thoughts from the Lord. Brad and Terry brought enthusiasm for walking with God—and it was contagious.

✓ If you were to give out a discipleship bulldog award in your group, to whom would you give it? Why?

✓ How well are the group members doing in encouraging one another and holding each other accountable for Quiet Times and verses each week? Give your group a grade A+ to F-. Be ready to share your thoughts why.

✓ Go back and read the *My Commitment* pledge (page 22) you made at the beginning. What will need to change for you personally to be more of a bulldog?

How We Grow
as Christians

Whenever your Quiet Time gets dry, as it will from time to time, go back to the basics:

1. Get your pen in hand. Underline something important that speaks to you.
2. Ask the questions or emphasize different words.
3. Rewrite the verse in your own words.

The mechanics of your Quiet Time are like the skills of blocking, tackling, and reviewing the plays in football. When a team is not doing well, the coach always goes back to the basics. *Remember, part of your dry time is the Enemy trying to put a stumbling block in your path as you develop this new lifelong habit.* If this part of your Christian life is stopped, you cannot bear fruit. That's the Enemy's objective.

✓ How have you seen the Enemy work against you in your Quiet Time?

The process of Christian growth sometimes looks like a stock market chart. It goes up, then down, then hopefully higher. God understands this growth process and uses it to bring us to maturity.

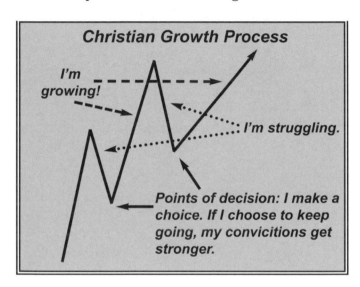

From God's perspective, coming to maturity means I stand on my own convictions. I do what's right because I believe the Lord wants me to do this, no matter what others do or say.

Paul said, *"[Timothy,] continue in what you have learned and become convinced of . . ."* (2 Timothy 3:14, emphasis added). God does not want you to do things just because someone tells you to. That's for children. But coming to maturity means you do something based on what *you have learned and become convinced of—for you.*

Here's where God steps in. Let's say you are struggling to have a Quiet Time, love your wife when she is unlovable, or tithe when you'd rather buy a new grill. *It's in the process of this struggle that decisions are made, convictions are born, and growth takes place.* If you don't choose right, the growth process stops. If you choose right, you continue to mature.

✓ Discuss the chart on page 90. What thoughts do you have about how we grow as Christians? What *Points of Decisions* have you already made in this course?

LEADERS LEAD

At the beginning of this course we laid out the value of skills. Your skill level in Quiet Time, meditating on the Scripture, and prayer has gone up. Now we want to add an additional skill to your leadership development process. We want you to begin to *lead the study.*

For the last few months you have watched your leader refer to his Leader's Guide from the beginning of the lesson and lead the study. Some of you may have used yours as well and followed along. Now we want to begin rotating the leading of the study. We have two books left and depending on the size of your group you should each be able to lead the lesson two or three times before the course ends.

Your leader will now step back and become just one of the group. His only role is to make sure that each of you knows when it is your turn to lead, continue to pray for each of you, and model the Quiet Time, Scripture memory verses, and lesson prep.

We want you to see that you can do this and prepare you to lead a study in your church in the future, perhaps next fall. If this course has had an impact on you, then you will want that impact to multiply to other men in your church or to the men around you.

✓ Read the *Successful Study Guidelines for EVERY MAN A WARRIOR* on the next page. Jot down at least two issues to discuss with the group on how to improve the study.

✓ Leader: As a group read page 92 together before you discuss the above question.

SUCCESSFUL STUDY GUIDELINES FOR EVERY MAN A WARRIOR

A successful group study normally includes the following:

☛ Start on Time. Usually there is a time of catching up at the beginning, but try to start within five minutes from the stated time.

☛ Review verses together each week. In some groups the men just pair off as they arrive to start reviewing their verses. If someone arrives late have him review verses with the leader after the study. (See Ecclesiastes 4:9-10.)

☛ Shares Quiet Times each week. Follow the format for sharing Quiet Times on page 35.

☛ As a group try to have your verses reviewed, Completion Record updated and your Quiet Times shared within thirty minutes of starting.

☛ Everyone has the lesson done and is prepared to share.

☛ The leader helps everyone to participate by asking those whot are quieter to share their answers or thoughts.

☛ The leader keeps watch on the time so that the group does not need to rush through the last part of the study in order to end on time.

☛ Keep the group on track. When the group has gone off on a tangent, the leader says, *"Okay let's go back to the study."*

☛ As the course progresses the lessons get longer. Each of you will invest considerable time to study and prepare for these lessons. As a group, hold each other accountable to keep the discussion on the lesson.

☛ End on time. If you started the study at 7:10 then end by 8:40 (90 minutes). Then men can stick around and talk as long as they want.

☛ If the interest and discussion on a lesson is especially long, it is okay to take a second week on that lesson. Sometimes this can help members get caught up.

☛ Pray together as a group each week using the *WAR* method of prayer.

☛ Give grace to people who are experiencing unusual circumstances at work or at home.

☛ The group is a safe place to share your struggles. Personal issues shared in the group are kept in confidence.

Here is a trustworthy saying: If anyone sets his heart on being [a leader] he desires a noble task. (1 Timothy 3:1author paraphrase).

✓ Leader, hand out the next book in the *EVERY MAN A WARRIOR* series. Ask for volunteers (or assign) who will lead the lessons in the next book. Jot their names next to the lesson titles in the Table of Contents.

PROFICIENCY EVALUATION
Lessons 1 – 8

First try to fill in the answers without looking. Then review Lessons 1–8 to find and check your answers. Hint: The questions go in the same order as the lessons.

✓ Why is it that many Christian men do not finish life well?

✓ What is the first Building Block of Discipleship? What is the skill that goes with this block?

✓ What do the three letters in the *ABCs of Quiet Time* stand for?
A—

B—

C—

✓ What are some of the questions you should ask during the "A" part of your Quiet Time to help you meditate on a passage?

✓ Why is "B" the most important part?

✓ What are three reasons men fail in their Quiet Time?
1.

2.

3.

✓ What is the cause of spiritual fruitfulness, according to John 15:4-8?

✓ What are the most effective teaching methods that develop your walk with Christ?

✓ Why do we say the reference before and after reciting the verse?

✓ What is the second Building Block of Discipleship? What skills are needed to develop this?

✓ Meditation is the art of _____.

✓ What are some conditions for answered prayer?

✓ What do the letters *WAR* stand for when describing how to pray?

✓ What is the connection between loving God and obeying God?

✓ One great secret in discipleship is that *"Developing your love relationship with God causes you to _____."*

✓ The most fundamental reason to read, study, listen, or memorize the Scripture is so that you can _____.

No discipline seems pleasant at the time, but painful. Later on, however, it produces a harvest of righteousness and peace for those who have been trained by it.

—Hebrews 12:11

✓ Meditate on Hebrews 12:11 using the *Emphasize Different Words* method. Jot down which words you emphasized and how it affects the meaning of the verse.

✓ How does this verse relate to being a bulldog?

✓ Rewrite Hebrews 12:11 in your own words below.

Points to Remember

1. For a group to survive and true discipleship to take root, it needs at least one or two discipleship bulldogs. These men set the pace in having Quiet Times, memorizing verses, doing the lessons, and encouraging their brothers.

2. Growing to spiritual maturity means I develop my own convictions. Spiritual convictions are normally formed when I'm struggling, yet choose to do what's right.

3. A truly successful discipleship group has high standards. You will each invest considerable time to prepare your lesson. Successful groups maximize the time by starting and ending on schedule and keeping the group on target when discussing the lesson.

4. Successful discipleship groups see the spiritual disciplines of sharing Quiet Times and reviewing verses each week as an essential aspect of growing as a Christian.

Congratulations! You have just finished Book 1 of the EVERY MAN A WARRIOR series. If you have faithfully finished the lessons, learned the verses, and been regular in your Quiet Time, then you are becoming not only a warrior, but a leader as well. God has His hand on your life and wants to use you in the lives of other men.

Next week you will start Book 2 for those who are married. Book 3, if you are single and want to jump over Book 2. If you have a mixed group of married and single men, go to Book 2. Many single men want to study the topics of Marriage and Raising Children also.

EVERY MAN A WARRIOR

ASSIGNMENT FOR NEXT WEEK

1. Place Hebrews 12:11 in the front window of your *EMAW Verse Pack* and memorize it this week.

2. Come with your lesson prepared and ready to share.

✓ End in group prayer using the WAR method. Follow the pattern outlined on page 75 and the Leader's Guide instructions on page 70.

APPENDIX

Quiet Time Journal

Course Requirements

Contact Information

About the Author

THE
EVERY MAN A WARRIOR
ICON

The EVERY MAN A WARRIOR icon is a symbol of a man's Quiet Time. God intended for you to be a warrior that worships the person of Jesus Christ. Your Quiet Time is a place of worship; but also a place to get ready for battle. Make it your objective to spend enough time with Jesus each day to do both; worship and prepare for war. Each is an important part of who you are as a man.

I Am a Warrior and I Kneel at the Cross

I kneel at the cross, battered and bruised, with blood on my sword and a shield that is used. My helmet is off, my face is scarred. I'm weary and tired. I'm a warrior and I kneel at the cross.

I am also a prince and a son of the King, with power and authority to rule. But instead, I give up my life to serve because I'm a warrior and I kneel at the cross.

I live as a light in a dark world of pain. I fight to set captives free from their prison and shame. I battle for truth and I count the cost. I'm a warrior and I kneel at the cross.

I reject the world with its brokenness and loss, because He died for me upon that cross. Now I have HOPE and a lasting reward. I'm a warrior and I kneel at the cross.

I'm coming home soon when my battles are won. To see my father's face and hear, "Well done my son. You are home at last, take your place at my side; because I chose you to be a warrior and you knelt at the cross."

Lonnie Berger

Date_____ Passage I Read Today_____

Major themes from all I read.

_____

_____

Ask Questions

Is there:

A command to obey

A promise to claim

A sin to avoid

An application to make

Something new about God

Ask: Who, What, When, Where, Why

Emphasize:
Different words

Rewrite:
In your own words

Best verse and thought for the day. (Write the verse & your thoughts.)

_____

_____

_____

_____

_____

_____

_____

_____

_____

_____

Communicate With God

W - *Worship Him*

A - *Admit Sin*

R - *My Requests*

Date_____ Passage I Read Today_____

Major themes from all I read.

_____

_____

Ask Questions

Is there:

A command to obey

A promise to claim

A sin to avoid

An application to make

Something new about God

Ask: Who, What, When, Where, Why

Emphasize:
Different words

Rewrite:
In your own words

Best verse and thought for the day. (Write the verse & your thoughts.)

_____

_____

_____

_____

_____

_____

_____

_____

_____

Communicate With God

W - *Worship Him*

A - *Admit Sin*

R - *My Requests*

Date_____ Passage I Read Today_____

Major themes from all I read.

Ask Questions

Is there:

A command to obey

A promise to claim

A sin to avoid

An application to make

Something new about God

Ask: Who, What, When, Where, Why

Emphasize:
Different words

Rewrite:
In your own words

Best verse and thought for the day. (Write the verse & your thoughts.)

Communicate
With God

W - *Worship Him*

A - *Admit Sin*

R - *My Requests*

Date_____ Passage I Read Today_____

Major themes from all I read.

Ask Questions

Is there:

A command to obey

A promise to claim

A sin to avoid

An application to make

Something new about God

Ask: Who, What, When, Where, Why

Emphasize:
Different words

Rewrite:
In your own words

Best verse and thought for the day. (Write the verse & your thoughts.)

Communicate
With God

W - *Worship Him*

A - *Admit Sin*

R - *My Requests*

Date_____ Passage I Read Today_____

Major themes from all I read.

_____

_____

_____

Best verse and thought for the day. (Write the verse & your thoughts.)

_____

_____

_____

_____

_____

_____

_____

_____

_____

Ask Questions

Is there:

A command to obey

A promise to claim

A sin to avoid

An application to make

Something new about God

Ask: Who, What, When, Where, Why

Emphasize:
Different words

Rewrite:
In your own words

Communicate
With God
W - *Worship Him*
A - *Admit Sin*
R - *My Requests*

Date_____ Passage I Read Today_____

Major themes from all I read.

_____

_____

_____

Best verse and thought for the day. (Write the verse & your thoughts.)

_____

_____

_____

_____

_____

_____

_____

_____

_____

Ask Questions

Is there:

A command to obey

A promise to claim

A sin to avoid

An application to make

Something new about God

Ask: Who, What, When, Where, Why

Emphasize:
Different words

Rewrite:
In your own words

Communicate
With God
W - *Worship Him*
A - *Admit Sin*
R - *My Requests*

Date_____ Passage I Read Today_____

Major themes from all I read.

_____

_____

_____

Ask Questions

Is there:

A command to obey

A promise to claim

A sin to avoid

An application to make

Something new about God

Ask: Who, What, When, Where, Why

Emphasize:
Different words

Rewrite:
In your own words

Best verse and thought for the day. (Write the verse & your thoughts.)

_____

_____

_____

_____

_____

_____

_____

_____

Communicate
With God
W - *Worship Him*
A - *Admit Sin*
R - *My Requests*

Date_____ Passage I Read Today_____

Major themes from all I read.

_____

_____

_____

Ask Questions

Is there:

A command to obey

A promise to claim

A sin to avoid

An application to make

Something new about God

Ask: Who, What, When, Where, Why

Emphasize:
Different words

Rewrite:
In your own words

Best verse and thought for the day. (Write the verse & your thoughts.)

_____

_____

_____

_____

_____

_____

_____

_____

Communicate
With God
W - *Worship Him*
A - *Admit Sin*
R - *My Requests*

Date_____ Passage I Read Today_____
Major themes from all I read.
_____
_____
_____

Ask Questions

Is there:

A command to obey

A promise to claim

A sin to avoid

An application to make

Something new about God

Ask: Who, What, When, Where, Why

Emphasize:
Different words

Rewrite:
In your own words

Best verse and thought for the day. (Write the verse & your thoughts.)
_____
_____
_____
_____
_____
_____
_____
_____
_____

Communicate
With God
W - Worship Him
A - Admit Sin
R - My Requests

Date_____ Passage I Read Today_____
Major themes from all I read.
_____
_____
_____

Ask Questions

Is there:

A command to obey

A promise to claim

A sin to avoid

An application to make

Something new about God

Ask: Who, What, When, Where, Why

Emphasize:
Different words

Rewrite:
In your own words

Best verse and thought for the day. (Write the verse & your thoughts.)
_____
_____
_____
_____
_____
_____
_____
_____
_____

Communicate
With God
W - Worship Him
A - Admit Sin
R - My Requests

Date_____ Passage I Read Today_____

Major themes from all I read.

_____

_____

_____

Ask Questions

Is there:

A command to obey

A promise to claim

A sin to avoid

An application to make

Something new about God

Ask: Who, What, When, Where, Why

Emphasize:
Different words

Rewrite:
In your own words

Best verse and thought for the day. (Write the verse & your thoughts.)

_____

_____

_____

_____

_____

_____

_____

_____

Communicate
With God

W - *Worship Him*

A - *Admit Sin*

R - *My Requests*

Date_____ Passage I Read Today_____

Major themes from all I read.

_____

_____

_____

Ask Questions

Is there:

A command to obey

A promise to claim

A sin to avoid

An application to make

Something new about God

Ask: Who, What, When, Where, Why

Emphasize:
Different words

Rewrite:
In your own words

Best verse and thought for the day. (Write the verse & your thoughts.)

_____

_____

_____

_____

_____

_____

_____

_____

Communicate
With God

W - *Worship Him*

A - *Admit Sin*

R - *My Requests*

Date_____ Passage I Read Today_____

Major themes from all I read.

_____

_____

_____

Ask Questions

Is there:

A command to obey

A promise to claim

A sin to avoid

An application to make

Something new about God

Ask: Who, What, When, Where, Why

Emphasize:
Different words

Rewrite:
In your own words

Best verse and thought for the day. (Write the verse & your thoughts.)

_____

_____

_____

_____

_____

_____

_____

_____

Communicate
With God

W - *Worship Him*

A - *Admit Sin*

R - *My Requests*

Date_____ Passage I Read Today_____

Major themes from all I read.

_____

_____

_____

Ask Questions

Is there:

A command to obey

A promise to claim

A sin to avoid

An application to make

Something new about God

Ask: Who, What, When, Where, Why

Emphasize:
Different words

Rewrite:
In your own words

Best verse and thought for the day. (Write the verse & your thoughts.)

_____

_____

_____

_____

_____

_____

_____

_____

Communicate
With God

W - *Worship Him*

A - *Admit Sin*

R - *My Requests*

Date _____ Passage I Read Today _____
Major themes from all I read.

Ask Questions

Is there:

A command to obey

A promise to claim

A sin to avoid

An application to make

Something new about God

Ask: Who, What, When, Where, Why

Emphasize:
Different words

Rewrite:
In your own words

Best verse and thought for the day. (Write the verse & your thoughts.)

Communicate With God
W - Worship Him
A - Admit Sin
R - My Requests

Date _____ Passage I Read Today _____
Major themes from all I read.

Ask Questions

Is there:

A command to obey

A promise to claim

A sin to avoid

An application to make

Something new about God

Ask: Who, What, When, Where, Why

Emphasize:
Different words

Rewrite:
In your own words

Best verse and thought for the day. (Write the verse & your thoughts.)

Communicate With God
W - Worship Him
A - Admit Sin
R - My Requests

Date_____ Passage I Read Today_____

Major themes from all I read.

_____

_____

_____

Best verse and thought for the day. (Write the verse & your thoughts.)

_____

_____

_____

_____

_____

_____

_____

_____

_____

_____

_____

Ask Questions

Is there:

A command to obey

A promise to claim

A sin to avoid

An application to make

Something new about God

Ask: Who, What, When, Where, Why

Emphasize:
Different words

Rewrite:
In your own words

Communicate
With God

W - *Worship Him*

A - *Admit Sin*

R - *My Requests*

Date_____ Passage I Read Today_____

Major themes from all I read.

_____

_____

_____

Best verse and thought for the day. (Write the verse & your thoughts.)

_____

_____

_____

_____

_____

_____

_____

_____

_____

_____

_____

Ask Questions

Is there:

A command to obey

A promise to claim

A sin to avoid

An application to make

Something new about God

Ask: Who, What, When, Where, Why

Emphasize:
Different words

Rewrite:
In your own words

Communicate
With God

W - *Worship Him*

A - *Admit Sin*

R - *My Requests*

Date_____ Passage I Read Today_____

Major themes from all I read.

_____

_____

_____

Ask Questions

Is there:

A command to obey

A promise to claim

A sin to avoid

An application to make

Something new about God

Ask: Who, What, When, Where, Why

Emphasize:
Different words

Rewrite:
In your own words

Best verse and thought for the day. (Write the verse & your thoughts.)

_____

_____

_____

_____

_____

_____

_____

_____

_____

Communicate
With God
W - *Worship Him*
A - *Admit Sin*
R - *My Requests*

Date_____ Passage I Read Today_____

Major Themes from all I read.

_____

_____

_____

Ask Questions

Is there:

A command to obey

A promise to claim

A sin to avoid

An application to make

Something new about God

Ask: Who, What, When, Where, Why

Emphasize:
Different words

Rewrite:
In your own words

Best verse and thought for the day. (Write the verse & your thoughts.)

_____

_____

_____

_____

_____

_____

_____

_____

_____

Communicate
With God
W - *Worship Him*
A - *Admit Sin*
R - *My Requests*

Date_____ Passage I Read Today_____
Major themes from all I read.
_____

Ask Questions

Is there:

A command to obey

A promise to claim

A sin to avoid

An application to make

Something new about God

Ask: Who, What, When, Where, Why

Emphasize:
Different words

Rewrite:
In your own words

Best verse and thought for the day. (Write the verse & your thoughts.)
_____
_____
_____
_____
_____

Communicate *With God*
W - *Worship Him*
A - *Admit Sin*
R - *My Requests*
_____

Date_____ Passage I Read Today_____
Major themes from all I read.
_____

Ask Questions

Is there:

A command to obey

A promise to claim

A sin to avoid

An application to make

Something new about God

Ask: Who, What, When, Where, Why

Emphasize:
Different words

Rewrite:
In your own words

Best verse and thought for the day. (Write the verse & your thoughts.)
_____
_____
_____
_____
_____

Communicate *With God*
W - *Worship Him*
A - *Admit Sin*
R - *My Requests*
_____

Date_____ Passage I Read Today_____

Major themes from all I read.

Ask Questions

Is there:

A command to obey

A promise to claim

A sin to avoid

An application to make

Something new about God

Ask: Who, What, When, Where, Why

Emphasize:
Different words

Rewrite:
In your own words

Best verse and thought for the day. (Write the verse & your thoughts.)

Communicate
With God
W - *Worship Him*
A - *Admit Sin*
R - *My Requests*

Date_____ Passage I Read Today_____

Major themes from all I read.

Ask Questions

Is there:

A command to obey

A promise to claim

A sin to avoid

An application to make

Something new about God

Ask: Who, What, When, Where, Why

Emphasize:
Different words

Rewrite:
In your own words

Best verse and thought for the day. (Write the verse & your thoughts.)

Communicate
With God
W - *Worship Him*
A - *Admit Sin*
R - *My Requests*

Date_____ Passage I Read Today_____

Major themes from all I read.

Ask Questions

Is there:

A command to obey

A promise to claim

A sin to avoid

An application to make

Something new about God

Ask: Who, What, When, Where, Why

Emphasize:
Different words

Rewrite:
In your own words

Best verse and thought for the day. (Write the verse & your thoughts.)

Communicate With God

W - *Worship Him*

A - *Admit Sin*

R - *My Requests*

Date_____ Passage I Read Today_____

Major themes from all I read.

Ask Questions

Is there:

A command to obey

A promise to claim

A sin to avoid

An application to make

Something new about God

Ask: Who, What, When, Where, Why

Emphasize:
Different words

Rewrite:
In your own words

Best verse and thought for the day. (Write the verse & your thoughts.)

Communicate With God

W - *Worship Him*

A - *Admit Sin*

R - *My Requests*

Date_____ Passage I Read Today_____

Major themes from all I read.
_____
_____
_____

Ask Questions

Is there:

A command to obey

A promise to claim

A sin to avoid

An application to make

Something new about God

Ask: Who, What, When, Where, Why

Emphasize:
Different words

Rewrite:
In your own words

Best verse and thought for the day. (Write the verse & your thoughts.)
_____
_____
_____
_____
_____
_____
_____
_____

Communicate With God

W - Worship Him

A - Admit Sin

R - My Requests

Date_____ Passage I Read Today_____

Major Themes from all I read.
_____
_____
_____

Ask Questions

Is there:

A command to obey

A promise to claim

A sin to avoid

An application to make

Something new about God

Ask: Who, What, When, Where, Why

Emphasize:
Different words

Rewrite:
In your own words

Best verse and thought for the day. (Write the verse & your thoughts.)
_____
_____
_____
_____
_____
_____
_____
_____

Communicate With God

W - Worship Him

A - Admit Sin

R - My Requests

Date_____ Passage I Read Today_____
Major themes from all I read.
_____

_____

Best verse and thought for the day. (Write the verse & your thoughts.)

Ask Questions

Is there:

A command to obey

A promise to claim

A sin to avoid

An application to make

Something new about God

Ask: Who, What, When, Where, Why

Emphasize:
Different words

Rewrite:
In your own words

Communicate
With God
W - *Worship Him*
A - *Admit Sin*
R - *My Requests*

Date_____ Passage I Read Today_____
Major themes from all I read.
_____

_____

Best verse and thought for the day. (Write the verse & your thoughts.)

Ask Questions

Is there:

A command to obey

A promise to claim

A sin to avoid

An application to make

Something new about God

Ask: Who, What, When, Where, Why

Emphasize:
Different words

Rewrite:
In your own words

Communicate
With God
W - *Worship Him*
A - *Admit Sin*
R - *My Requests*

Date _____ Passage I Read Today _____ _____

Major themes from all I read.

_____

_____

_____

Ask Questions

Is there:

A command to obey

A promise to claim

A sin to avoid

An application to make

Something new about God

Ask: Who, What, When, Where, Why

Emphasize:
Different words

Rewrite:
In your own words

Best verse and thought for the day. (Write the verse & your thoughts.)

_____

_____

_____

_____

_____

_____

_____

_____

Communicate
With God
W - *Worship Him*
A - *Admit Sin*
R - *My Requests*

Date _____ Passage I Read Today _____ _____

Major themes from all I read.

_____

_____

_____

Ask Questions

Is there:

A command to obey

A promise to claim

A sin to avoid

An application to make

Something new about God

Ask: Who, What, When, Where, Why

Emphasize:
Different words

Rewrite:
In your own words

Best verse and thought for the day. (Write the verse & your thoughts.)

_____

_____

_____

_____

_____

_____

_____

_____

Communicate
With God
W - *Worship Him*
A - *Admit Sin*
R - *My Requests*

Date_____ Passage I Read Today_____

Major themes from all I read.
_____

_____

_____

Ask Questions

Is there:

A command to obey

A promise to claim

A sin to avoid

An application to make

Something new about God

Ask: Who, What, When, Where, Why

Emphasize:
Different words

Rewrite:
In your own words

Best verse and thought for the day. (Write the verse & your thoughts.)
_____

_____

_____

_____

_____

_____

_____

_____

_____

_____

Communicate
With God
W - *Worship Him*
A - *Admit Sin*
R - *My Requests*

Date_____ Passage I Read Today_____

Major themes from all I read.
_____

_____

_____

Ask Questions

Is there:

A command to obey

A promise to claim

A sin to avoid

An application to make

Something new about God

Ask: Who, What, When, Where, Why

Emphasize:
Different words

Rewrite:
In your own words

Best verse and thought for the day. (Write the verse & your thoughts.)
_____

_____

_____

_____

_____

_____

_____

_____

_____

_____

Communicate
With God
W - *Worship Him*
A - *Admit Sin*
R - *My Requests*

Date_____ Passage I Read Today_____

Major themes from all I read.
_____
_____
_____

Ask Questions

Is there:

A command to obey

A promise to claim

A sin to avoid

An application to make

Something new about God

Ask: Who, What, When, Where, Why

Emphasize:
Different words

Rewrite:
In your own words

Best verse and thought for the day. (Write the verse & your thoughts.)
_____
_____
_____
_____
_____
_____

Communicate
With God
W - *Worship Him*
A - *Admit Sin*
R - *My Requests*

Date_____ Passage I Read Today_____

Major themes from all I read.
_____
_____
_____

Ask Questions

Is there:

A command to obey

A promise to claim

A sin to avoid

An application to make

Something new about God

Ask: Who, What, When, Where, Why

Emphasize:
Different words

Rewrite:
In your own words

Best verse and thought for the day. (Write the verse & your thoughts.)
_____
_____
_____
_____
_____
_____

Communicate
With God
W - *Worship Him*
A - *Admit Sin*
R - *My Requests*

COMPLETION RECORD
Course Requirements for Book 1

This course is designed for men who want to become the man God wants them to be. Change will only happen when we do the work and give it our best effort. *The Completion Record* is a tool designed to help you gauge your progress and help you encourage each other to succeed.

✓ Have another member of your group check you on the requirements of this course. Have them initial and date each item.

SCRIPTURE MEMORY RECORD

I have memorized and quoted word-perfect:

INITIAL - DATE

Matthew 22:36-38 _____

2 Timothy 3:16-17 _____

Joshua 1:8 _____

John 16:24 _____

Philippians 4:6-7 _____

James 1:22 _____

Hebrews 12:11 _____

Quoted the first six verses: _____

(You will not have Hebrews 12:11 yet.)

Book 1: Walking with God

Initial - Date

Lesson 1: *Why Discipleship?*   _____

Lesson 2: *Finding the "One Thing"*   _____

Lesson 3: *Why Men Fail*   _____

Lesson 4: *A Man of the Word*   _____

Lesson 5: *Meditation: Thinking with Purpose*   _____

Lesson 6: *You Do Not Have Because You Do Not Ask*   _____

Lesson 7: *The Real Purpose of Prayer*   _____

Lesson 8: *The Secret to a Changed Life*   _____

Lesson 9: *Every Man a Bulldog*   _____

Quiet Time Journal Record

Initial - Date

I have recorded ten Quiet Time sessions in my journal. _____

I have recorded twenty Quiet Time sessions in my journal. _____

Course Requirements for Completion of Book 1

• Finish all nine lessons.   _____

• Memorize and quote six Scripture passages.   _____

• Record twenty Quiet Times or more.   _____

Congratulations! You have finished Book 1 of this course.

Contact Information

Name .... E-mail ....

Address ....

Phone (H) .... (Cell) ....

Name .... E-mail ....

Address ....

Phone (H) .... (Cell) ....

Name .... E-mail ....

Address ....

Phone (H) .... (Cell) ....

Name .... E-mail ....

Address ....

Phone (H) .... (Cell) ....

Name .... E-mail ....

Address ....

Phone (H) .... (Cell) ....

Name .... E-mail ....

Address ....

Phone (H) .... (Cell) ....

Name .... E-mail ....

Address ....

Phone (H) .... (Cell) ....

NAME .... E-MAIL ....

ADDRESS ....

PHONE (H) .... (CELL) ....

NAME .... E-MAIL ....

ADDRESS ....

PHONE (H) .... (CELL) ....

NAME .... E-MAIL ....

ADDRESS ....

PHONE (H) .... (CELL) ....

NAME .... E-MAIL ....

ADDRESS ....

PHONE (H) .... (CELL) ....

NAME .... E-MAIL ....

ADDRESS ....

PHONE (H) .... (CELL) ....

NAME .... E-MAIL ....

ADDRESS ....

PHONE (H) .... (CELL) ....

NAME .... E-MAIL ....

ADDRESS ....

PHONE (H) .... (CELL) ....

ABOUT THE AUTHOR: LONNIE BERGER

Lonnie Berger has been on staff with The Navigators, an international Christian organization known for its expertise in discipleship and leadership development, for more than 30 years.

While in college at Kansas State University in Manhattan, Kansas, Mr. Berger received his initial Navigator ministry training. His first staff assignment was behind the Iron Curtain in communist Romania, where he lived and directed the Navigator work in three cities. There he met his missionary wife, June, also ministering in Romania with The Navigators. They have been married since 1984 and have two grown daughters, Stephanie and Karen.

During his years on staff with The Navigators, Mr. Berger has served as one of five U.S. Directors for the Community ministry, overseeing the development of 175 staff in 125 major cities. He is a conference speaker and continues mentoring other Christian leaders in discipleship, evangelism, ministry funding, and spiritual warfare.

www.EveryManAWarrior.com

Every Man a Warrior is a ministry of The Navigators.

GLEN EYRIE

Glen Eyrie Spiritual Retreats

Glen Eyrie offers an ongoing lineup of retreats for Men, Women, Couples, and Ministry Leaders. Our desire is for these retreats to strengthen the foundations of your faith and to cause you to go deeper in your relationship with God!

Please visit our website for information on different spiritual retreats you can attend, dates, costs, and availability.

www.gleneyrie.org/retreats

GLEN EYRIE
Christian Camps and Conferences